Heart of Worship

How To Live A Life That Reflects Your Allegiance To Jesus

Bryan Keller

HEART OF WORSHIP

Unless otherwise noted, scripture quotations are from The NIV® Bible (The Holy Bible, New International Version®) copyright © 1973, 1978, 1984, 2011 by Biblica, Inc.® Used by permission. All rights reserved worldwide.

Scripture quotations marked (ESV) are from The ESV® Bible (The Holy Bible, English Standard Version®), copyright © 2001 by Crossway, a publishing ministry of Good News Publishers. Used by permission. All rights reserved.

Scripture quotations marked (NLT) are taken from the Holy Bible, New Living Translation, copyright ©1996, 2004, 2015 by Tyndale House Foundation. Used by permission of Tyndale House Publishers, Carol Stream, Illinois 60188. All rights reserved.

Copyright © 2023 by Bryan Keller
All rights reserved.

Paperback Print ISBN: 979-8-9879563-2-8
Hardcover Print ISBN: 979-8-9879563-1-1
Ebook ISBN: 979-8-9879563-0-4

First Edition

No portion of this book may be reproduced in any form without written permission from the publisher or author, except as permitted by U.S. copyright law. For information regarding using content in this book for your ministry or if you need bulk copies, please reach out to me at:
message.heartofworship@gmail.com.

*"As water reflects the face,
so one's life reflects the heart."*

Proverbs 27:19

Table of Contents

Preface ix

Introduction xvii

1. Purpose 1
2. Made to Worship 9
3. How's Your Heart? 17
4. Heart On Fire 31
5. A Life Poured Out 49
6. Overflow 57
7. Calloused Hands 73
8. Spirit & Truth 91
9. Be Not Afraid 113
10. You Called My Name 133
11. Whole Hearted 153
12. The Challenge 173

Conclusion 189

Share The Love 192
Acknowledgements 195
About The Author 197
Other Notes 199

Preface

It is a sad reality that many people that call themselves Christians do not follow Christ.

In actuality, following Christ makes you a Christian.

This is a statement that I want to challenge you with early so that you may introspectively think through your own life as we look at Jesus' life. The word "Christian" comes from the Greek word Christianos (Χριστιανός) which simply means "follower of Christ" and is an identifier we first see in Acts 11 that the people of the world used to identify individuals who followed in the ways and teachings of Jesus Christ.

When Jesus is on the throne of your heart and you follow His ways, you are a Christian. That is a hard reality that I learned when looking at the throne of my heart in college and I saw myself still sitting there on the throne in pride and selfishness, even after having known Jesus for many years.

It wasn't until I had the courage to step off the throne and relinquish authority in my life to Jesus that I could, in good conscience, call myself a follower of Jesus. Not to say that before that moment, God was not working in my life. He was very much involved in forming my character and using the people in my life to instill wisdom and discernment into my brain, but it was not until I accepted Jesus' authority in my life as King and explored His teachings for myself that my heart, my mind, and my soul truly began transforming.

That is also not to say that once Jesus has the throne of your heart, you are smooth sailing for the rest of life. Trial and temptation will still attempt to tear you down, and may succeed at times. Pride and selfishness are still going to rear their ugly heads and try to convince you that your ways are better than the ways of Jesus. But being under the allegiance of Jesus brings faith, hope, and love, and being filled with His Spirit brings love, joy, and peace into your life - to name a few things of many.

So you know a bit about me. My name is Bryan Keller and I live in Atlanta, GA with my beautiful wife, sweet Sydney. I grew up with parents that taught me in the ways of the Lord, and God blessed me with community and mentors that poured into me as I grew into adulthood, to whom I am forever grateful.

The ones that know me best know that I have always been an observer. I watch and absorb first, try my best to filter through what I am observing, then decide or take action based on what I have learned. Even so, I have made destructive choices based on desire and touched the flame that I already knew was hot more than I would like to admit.

Throughout adolescence, I didn't truly consult God for my decisions or have a desire to live a life of obedience to God, but I tried to respect my parents and the rules they set because I trusted them.

But rules alone, out of obligation with no substantial "why" underneath, can lead to a legalistic mindset, which I began to develop from other authority figures who may not have been as wise in discipleship and discipline as my parents were. If legalism bleeds into your mindset when reading God's Word, the Bible, much of the beauty in His love letter to humanity is easy to miss. Eventually, I started to ask "why" more often and had big questions about God and the Bible. The good news is that God invites us to seek Him and He promises we will find Him when we seek Him with all of our heart.

When you blindly live without some of the big "whys" in life answered, chaos and frustration can emerge inside of you. As a metaphorical child in your faith that is learning and growing, you often have to rely on the teaching and leadership of those around you, like parents, but as you mature, you need to have discernment and the ability to apply the truths found in God's word to your own life.

> "When I was a child, I talked like a child, I thought like a child, I reasoned like a child. When I became a man, I put the ways of childhood behind me."
> 1 Corinthians 13:11

Early on, I didn't cling to the truths so lovingly available in scripture, and for me, living a "good" life became a balancing act with sin. I would get myself into situations that I knew I had conviction about, but not enough faith, boldness, or discipline to walk away from. I would tell myself "I am a pretty good person" or "It's really not that bad." And if you have ever told yourself one of those statements like I did, you already know what sort of mess that way of thinking will create in life.

So why couldn't I just figure out this whole faith thing? It was because I was initially looking in the wrong places. My religion and legalistic actions were the only things I was looking at to fix my heaven/hell situation. I had a very shallow relationship with God, and no real reason to live differently in my comfortable but unclear life. I didn't have a strong anthem for my life, or a genuine reason for my existence beyond having fun, being a good person, and striving for happiness. With this lack of clarity, I was stuck managing the sin in my life instead of living in the full freedom that Jesus wanted for me. You may resonate with a past story like that, or you might be somewhere in it right now, confused and frustrated.

Why is it so easy to live without being intentional in finding answers to our "whys?" Why is it so easy to be passive and allow life to fly by when we are called to zealously press into the truths we have discovered in God's Word?

We humans can clearly see a gaping hole in our hearts, yet it is so easy to settle for being incomplete. Or we may try to stuff the hole in our hearts with any temporary desire in sight. We might deny our incompleteness and run away from the clarity we once saw because it was too difficult to look at. We might run back to the murky waters of sin because it was easier to live with no boundaries in the grey area of right and wrong. Or we might just start coasting in life, living by default, lukewarm in faith with no desire to grow. To pose my question another way...

Why do we allow ourselves to live such a lacking life?

It's because when we allow the wrong things to lead our life,
we lack true purpose.

But that does not have to be the case. There is a purpose worthy of the one life you have been given on this earth to live. A purpose worth living for and dying for. A purpose that fills any void, that fully satisfies. The truth is that we need more followers of Jesus to step into their God given purpose to help bring the kingdom of heaven to earth, and leave behind the idols that have crept so sneakily into the hearts of many.

I am excited that you have decided to jump into this book and that you are willing to invest time into deepening your relationship with Jesus. While writing this book, God is continuing to work on my heart, and it has been a joy and challenge to get these words onto paper for you. I have asked Jesus that it is not my words that you hold on to, but His, because my words alone will fall flat while God's Word brings life to the full.

My **goal** in writing this book is that it creates clarity for you as we look at Jesus' words to His people.

My **aim** is that as we look at Jesus' words, they will challenge and change our hearts and bring to light the areas of our souls that have been hidden in the dark for too long.

My **hope** is that as we see Jesus' life and the truthful words in scripture, we will align our hearts to God's will and act upon His words to us. That as the Church, the body of Christ, we will unify and allow God to use our lives for His glory. That as warriors of Christ, we will get off the sidelines and hop into the battle of faith against a very real enemy who is trying everything he can to lull you to sleep or take you out.

My **prayer** is that this book will not only challenge you, but encourage you to take another bold step of faith with Jesus, no matter where you are on your journey with Him, and that Jesus will further soften your heart to the world around you as He, and His will, becomes your ultimate desire.

Your ultimate worship.

Take Up Your Cross and Follow Jesus

"Then Jesus told his disciples.
'If anyone would come after me, let him deny himself and take up his cross and follow me. For whoever would save his life will lose it, but whoever loses his life for my sake will find it.'"
Matthew 16:24-25 ESV

*Throughout Heart Of Worship, I have commonly capitalized pronouns when referring to God the Father, Jesus, and the Holy Spirit to create clarity in my writing.

Introduction
Seeking & Finding

The first big question: **"Why do I exist?"**

Have you ever had a thought like that? Most people ask a question like this one at some point in life, and often it is these types of questions that get people thinking about, and looking for, something bigger than themselves.

You know those people who radiate fullness and love from their life? In their expression and actions, in the way they light up a room with their presence, there is just something different about them. I wanted a life like that, and I soon found that the reason for their fullness started with their confidence in knowing who and, more importantly, whose they are. And knowing who, and whose, they are told them exactly why they existed.

In any faith or religion, there are always fundamental explanations trying to answer the big questions in life, trying to explain your purpose. And when you have grasped clarity on the true answers to the big life-altering questions, you further understand your purposeful "why" which will direct you and give you confidence in the roots of your life. Because at the core of humans, we want truth, we want purpose, we want clarity, and we want confidence in our beliefs.

Most religious beliefs are based on the fact that you have to live a "good" or "right" life so that you may enter some kind of pleasant afterlife when you die because of your good works on earth. But Christianity is set apart from every other religion on the planet because it is based on the humble fact that we could do nothing on our own to live a sinless, blameless life, worthy of being in the presence of God. We accept that we could never attain such holiness on our own, so God made a way.

> "For it is by grace you have been saved, through faith—and this is not from yourselves, it is the gift of God— not by works, so that no one can boast."
> Ephesians 2:8-9

To align with Christianity is to believe, with faith, that the God of Israel, the Creator of everything, is the one true God that sent His only son, Jesus—God in flesh and blood,

from heaven to earth to willingly give His life on a cross and take on the death penalty of our sin, so that you and I may be saved from eternal separation from God by accepting His invitation for eternal life in His presence, if only we repent, turn from our sin, and profess Jesus, as the Lord and Savior of our heart.

This is what it means to say yes to being a Christian, a follower of Christ, and if we accept His leadership in our lives, it will require faith in Jesus as our foundation. There are many concrete aspects of life that God reveals to us during our time on earth if we will press into His words and uncover His truths. In scripture, God speaks this promise through a prophet named Jeremiah:

> "You will seek me and find me when you seek me with all your heart."
> Jeremiah 29:13 NIV

For context, God is speaking through Jeremiah to give hope to all of His people who were exiled from their land, Jerusalem, in the midst of a rebellious downward spiral. The beauty is that the promise given to them is true for us today, too. If you seek after God with all your heart, you will find Him, and He will give you the clarity you are hungry for.

When you take up God on His promises and decide to truly live a life following Jesus, seeking after Him with all of your heart, you will most definitely find fullness sewn throughout your existence.

Following Jesus wholeheartedly could very well be the most difficult decision you ever make in your entire life, but the reward far outweighs any cost you may bear. Here in America, we have the freedom to accept Jesus' invitation to us with little persecution, but in many parts of the world, you could easily be sentenced to death for such an allegiance to Jesus. Even then, the eternal reward would still be worth the high cost of losing your life.

When you fully follow Jesus and proclaim Him as Lord and Savior over your entire life, you gain powerful clarity that unleashes peace all over your soul, and you begin to see your purpose unfold in the overarching story of creation. On the contrary, it is frustrating to live a life lacking clarity. A life where every decision is based on feeling, emotion, and desire. Not only is it extremely frustrating, but it can also be catastrophically dangerous.

All throughout scripture, we see a clear picture of what our lives are designed to look like as a follower of Jesus. God didn't just leave the core attributes of our lives to our own ambiguous imagination of what it is supposed to look like following Jesus.

Yes, each person has been crafted specifically and uniquely, but we see that God's fundamental architectural design for every human is to glorify and worship God as the Creator, Shepherd, and Savior of our lives. And God came down from His throne in heaven as Jesus so that He Himself could set an example for us to learn from and live by. What a beautiful act of grace from the loving Creator of you and me!

A big theme for this book is to peer into what it means to live a life of "worship" like we see in the book of Romans:

> "Therefore, I urge you, brothers and sisters, in view of God's mercy, to offer your bodies as a living sacrifice, holy and pleasing to God—**this is your true and proper worship.** Do not conform to the pattern of this world, but be transformed by the renewing of your mind. Then you will be able to test and approve what God's will is—his good, pleasing and perfect will."
> Romans 12:1-2

This book, Heart of Worship, is a great spot to learn more about Jesus' words and how to apply them to your life, but if you have not read the Bible all the way through yet, I strongly encourage you to put this book down and read the Bible cover-to-cover first. Come back to this book after you have digested God's words directly, with all the context. You can go to my Linktree (**https://linktr.ee/bryankeller** or scan QR code on the next page) to download a free chronological Bible reading plan that guides you through the entire Bible in one year. It is a great resource if you want to read the chronological narrative of God's love story to humanity.

If you do decide to read Heart Of Worship before reading the whole Bible, spend additional time digging into the verses of Scripture I reference so you can gain some clarity on the context of these Scriptures.

I mainly wrote Heart Of Worship to emphasize God's original design for your life and to proclaim and highlight what He has already spoken through His perfect Word to you. This book will pale in comparison to the holy Word of God, but I hope it assists you in your walk with Jesus by connecting some dots that you may have not connected before.

If you have been following Jesus for a while now but feel like something is missing in your life, or if you want to be challenged to dig deeper into your relationship with Jesus, this book is for you. Jesus wants to speak to you and He wants to know you personally. He wants you to respond to the words He has spoken to you, and He wants you to live in confidence rooted in His goodness. I hope that the stories and scriptural truths uncovered in this book will give you a better understanding of your relationship with Jesus so that you can live a life on fire for Jesus, filled with a joyful heart of worship.

At the end of each chapter, I have listed some worship songs that inspire me regarding each chapter. I would encourage you to absorb each chapter, one at a time, without rushing, then sit in a time of worship with Jesus. Feel free to use the "Heart Of Worship" playlist I created for you as you process each chapter. By scanning the QR code on with your smartphone camera app or by going to my Linktree (**https://linktr.ee/bryankeller**), you can get to and save the playlist on Spotify, Apple Music, YouTube Music, and Amazon Music. After each chapter, just listen to a few songs with Jesus. Let the Lord reveal new things about Himself to you and ask Him to speak to you. Create space to hear His voice in your life.

I have also made an instrumental worship song playlist called "Heart of Worship - Instrumental" that I like to listen to while I read or work since it puts my mind at peace that you can find at the link/QR code as well:

Scan QR Code Here:

Read, reflect on thoughts you may have, and most importantly, talk with your Creator. God has His ear open to you and is eager to spend time with you. Dig deeper into the scriptures I reference. Spend time in prayer, listen and be attentive to what God is putting on your heart, and proclaim the truths of Jesus in musical worship and singing!

Share truths you discover with your community. Wrestle with the tough ones and find a friend to grow alongside with and share revelations with. Allow yourself time to digest and process as you read **so that you can ultimately take action on what truths God reveals to you**.

With the throne of your heart open to Jesus, get ready to jump into the plans God has for your life as you begin to further position your heart of worship directly towards the King of kings - the Messiah and Savior of humanity, Jesus Christ the Nazarene.

> "[1]Now faith is confidence in what we hope for and assurance about what we do not see... [6]And without faith it is impossible to please God, because anyone who comes to him must believe that he exists and that he rewards those who earnestly seek him."
> Hebrews 11:1 & 6

Chapter 1

Purpose

"Life with Jesus won't be easy, but it will always be worth it."

Living without a clear purpose is one of the most agonizing places to be, and during my first few years of college, I wrestled with figuring out what my purpose in life was. I didn't have the full picture yet, but I knew I wanted to glorify God with my life. I enjoyed creating things, and I found joy in adding value to other people's lives, so I joined the business school. A few semesters into my education, I soon found myself in the Coles College of Business to learn the ins and outs of how business works.

It was there that I heard a simple analogy that stuck with me, pointing out the importance of understanding purpose, and why it is essential to understand yours. It went something like this:

The iPhone, what an incredible invention. One thing that it is really great for is being an extraordinary paperweight! It's just the right weight and size to keep all of your papers pinned down to keep your desk neat and organized. It has a sleek and modern design and is made of the best materials you can find. It's quite possibly the best paperweight you can buy on the market right now!

We all know the iPhone, although it could be used as a remarkable paperweight, has so much more capability and functionality than pinning papers. Its purpose was not to be a paperweight. It was an innovation designed and created by Steve Jobs and Steve Wozniak to be a smartphone that allows users to have the internet in the palm of their hand, to allow anyone and everyone to connect with each other at any moment, and to be a tool filled with applications that assist you with everyday life.

It was after hearing this example in simple terms that something clicked in my brain. I knew I had a Creator, the Yahweh God, and I knew His Word had truths in it about my purpose. There were also many voices and pressures internally and externally, trying to tell me who I was or *should* be. I decided I should let my Creator, the one that designed me and knows how I operate to my fullest potential, be the dominant voice for determining my purpose.

Our lives can be scarily similar to the iPhone analogy. We have a God who has hand-crafted us for a distinct and powerful purpose. A purpose that can be a vehicle for radical life change in ourselves and every single person we encounter during our time on earth! A life purpose that many people may never truly realize or utilize because they settle for being an extraordinary paperweight.

Living with a clear and full purpose is frequently missed out on by people, even in the church, not because they didn't have a God-given purpose, but because they didn't live out their purpose.

When you accept Jesus into your life, you are proclaiming that His ways are better than yours. You are submitting your life and your plans to follow His plans for you, and you are recognizing and accepting His unconditional, overwhelming, never-ending love. Allowing Jesus to step onto the throne of your heart by allowing God to direct your steps is the only way you will ever be able to live out your God-given purpose to the full. He is the source of your life, a well that will never run dry, and His arms are the only place to find eternal purpose and peace for your soul.

> "Come to me, all you who are weary and burdened, and I will give you rest. Take my yoke upon you and learn from me, for I am gentle and humble in heart, and you will find rest for your souls."
> Matthew 11:28-29

Accepting Jesus' love and leadership in life is essential, and as you grow and develop a relationship with Him, there is a crucial pillar that needs to be included in the bedrock of your decision to continue to follow Him every single day – the commitment to recognize and live out your purpose.

In Genesis 1, God created the heavens and earth, the land and the sea, and all the creatures of the earth. The Bible says that God simply spoke them into existence. He literally said, "Let there be light!" and BOOM, light was created. He spoke into existence the heavens and earth, the sun and moon, the stars, the land and sea, even the birds, fish, and animals. But then He comes to man.

God makes all the things of the earth using nothing but His voice and then Genesis 2 says He formed man out of the dust of the ground and breathed the breath of life into man. He uses His creative craftsmanship to mold man uniquely, but the most remarkable statement about Genesis 1 and 2 is that God says He created man in the image of Himself. How incredible is it we are each made in the image of God!

> "Then God said, "Let us make mankind in our image, in our likeness, so that they may rule over the fish in the sea and the birds in the sky, over the livestock and all the wild animals, and over all the creatures that move along the ground."
> So God created mankind in his own image, in the image of God he created them; male and female he created them.
> God blessed them and said to them, "Be fruitful and increase in number; fill the earth and subdue it. Rule over the fish in the sea and the birds in the sky and over every living creature that moves on the ground."
> Genesis 1:26-28

Also, notice that in that section of Genesis, God gave man the responsibility of taking care of what He created. God tells Adam to tend to the earth, give names to the animals, and to be fruitful and multiply. That's a direct "how" of Adam's created purpose, but why did God tell Adam to do those things?

Although it was important to tend to the earth, to name the animals, and to grow the human population, **Adam's reason for existence, and deeply rooted purpose, was to glorify God and to worship Him through joyful relationship.**

As followers of Jesus, we are called to that same purpose every single day of our lives. It is a purpose that calls us to pour out everything we have for Him. To pour out our hearts, our desires, our plans, our finances, our relationships, our entire lives at the Lord's feet and allow Him to take control of everything, for our own good and His beautiful glory.

Jesus, God made man, calls us to align our lives and our plans with His ways and His plans while reassuring us that, although it will not be easy, it will be worth it. When you follow God's designed purpose for you, to worship Him however that may look like in your life, you get to experience a relationship with the Creator of YOU, and you get to fully live out your original design with joy and fullness.

Throughout scripture, God's living breathing Word, we see God validate what He says about you and me. Through stories, people, and examples of the past, we gain insight into God's plan for our lives today and for our future. We see His intention for our hearts to be lit on fire through a fervent desire to glorify His name. To experience peace and joy that comes from a full heart. To find community and to link arms with others we care for as we move on mission together. And to use our gifts to extend God's glory to others.

Sometimes we are too quick to jump to the specific "whats" of our individual life before accurately framing our purpose with our main "why?"

We serve a worthy God, and He has big plans to come for us. We just need to listen for and be ready to respond to His calling and commands for our lives.

And what is Jesus' promise to us for living a life fully trusted in the magnificent plans of God? A life filled with perfect peace, and an eternity that is built on the everlasting rock.

> "You keep him in perfect peace whose mind is stayed on you, because he trusts in you.
> Trust in the Lord forever, for the Lord God is an everlasting rock."
> Isaiah 26:3-4 ESV

Build Your House on the Rock

"Everyone then who hears these words of mine and does them will be like a wise man who built his house on the rock. And the rain fell, and the floods came, and the winds blew and beat on that house, but it did not fall, because it had been founded on the rock.

And everyone who hears these words of mine and does not do them will be like a foolish man who built his house on the sand. And the rain fell, and the floods came, and the winds blew and beat against that house, and it fell, and great was the fall of it."

Matthew 7:24-27

Chapter 1 - Songs

What A Beautiful Name, by: Hillsong Worship, Brooke Ligertwood

O Come to the Altar, by: Elevation Worship

Worthy Of Your Name, by: Passion, Sean Curran

Christ Be Magnified, by: Cody Carnes

Chapter 2

Made to Worship

"What are you worshiping?"

What do you think of when you hear the word "worship?" I initially think of Sunday mornings at church, where everyone gets to sing songs together. This form of worship creates space to connect to God through truth and celebrate Him as Lord. We get to sing scriptural truths, remind our hearts of God's goodness, and magnify Jesus through our voices and melodies.

The definition of worship is this: [1] **to show reverence and adoration towards something**.

It is easy to see a worship song as worship because it is clear adoration and reverence towards God, but Paul while writing Romans challenges us by saying that our entire lives are meant to be worship to Jesus.

---

1. Oxford Languages Dictionary, "worship"

A Living Sacrifice

"Therefore, I urge you, brothers and sisters, in view of God's mercy, to offer your bodies as a living sacrifice, holy and pleasing to God—this is your true and proper worship. Do not conform to the pattern of this world, but be transformed by the renewing of your mind. Then you will be able to test and approve what God's will is—his good, pleasing and perfect will."
Romans 12:1-2

Like a worship song, the way we conduct our lives are meant to magnify Jesus with fragrant adoration and admiration. As a musician, I absolutely love getting to worship our God through music, but it is so much deeper than that. Our entire life is worship! What we do, say, even think, is an act of worship. The real question we must then ask ourselves is this:

"What Am I Worshiping?"

Whether or not you follow Jesus, you are worshiping something: Success, achievement, freedom, independence, your spouse, children, friends, approval, money, a hobby or interest, another idol or god in your life, or more commonly... yourself. We are all naturally designed to align our life and effort in a direction for something. Whether our worship is pointed at something greater than ourselves, or to make something greater of ourselves, we all worship, and it is crucial to recognize what your life is pointing at.

When you submit to following Jesus, your whole life's aim turns from you or your idol(s) and toward **giving God glory**. Once our allegiance is pointed towards Jesus, our hobbies, jobs, relationships, and our whole lives are overflowing acts of worship that we are called to enjoy and excel at, all for God's glory.

So what are you worshiping?

For many years in Atlanta, I had the pleasure of being a part of a church called Passion City Church (PCC). The most incredible thing about PCC is the fact that they point to Jesus and worship Him in everything they do, and they do everything to the absolute best of their ability with excellence. You can tell when you walk into Passion City Church that they are intentional about glorifying God, as are many wonderful churches here in America and beyond.

Whether it is through a smiling face actually seeing you and greeting you at the door, through individuals praying over you or someone in need, through the pastor or another communicator bringing an incredible message, or through the beautiful musical worship, Jesus is central.

The leadership and team there listen closely to God's direction, then with faith, put their yes on the table for God to use them. Beyond that, they put in an immense amount of effort behind the scenes as God uses them to build His church and share Jesus with people around the world. That is how they glorify God, and they are so intent and passionate about what they do because they know why they do it and what they are created to do. Like any church, they have faults, since the church comprises imperfect humans like you and me, but they are intentional about making God known through their gifts, and that is profound.

We are called to do the same as individuals, and as a community, to glorify God with whatever gifts God has given to us to steward. He has given the gifts graciously, now it is up to us to use those gifts.

> "As each has received a gift, use it to serve one another, as good stewards of God's varied grace: whoever speaks, as one who speaks oracles of God; whoever serves, as one who serves by the strength that God supplies-in order that in everything God may be glorified through Jesus Christ. To him belong glory and dominion for-

ever and ever. Amen."
1 Peter 4:10 -11 ESV

In Matthew 25:14-30, Jesus speaks a parable about three servants that have been given various amounts of money from their master to steward while he is out of town. To summarize the story, the master praises the two servants that steward their gift well, by investing it, and they both have more to bring to their master upon his return. On the flip side, the third servant, with a smaller portion than the other two, hides his gift and does nothing with the gift he was given to steward. When the master returns and sees he did nothing with it, he is not pleased.

For us, God has given us all gifts and strengths, and of all the 8 billion people on this earth, He gave you distinct strengths and gifts to use for His glory. Whether you are a football player on your high school team, an architect in corporate America, a hard-working mom rasing up your kids, a CEO of a successful international tech company, or the kindest and most diligent server in the local restaurant, you have the ability to live your life as an act of worship to God, by stewarding the gifts God has given you excellently.

> "For I know the plans I have for you, declares the Lord, plans for peace and not for evil, to give you a future and a hope."
> Jeremiah 29:11 ESV

You have been placed precisely where you are for a distinct reason, and though you may not see it now, it is part of God's perfect plan for your life. A perfect plan meant for your good, and His glory.

> "And we know that in all things God works for the good of those who love him, who have been called according to his purpose."
> Romans 8:28

What incredible encouragement, even in the midst of difficulty. Yes, God's plans are for our good. But that does not mean we won't encounter pain, loss, and suffering during our lives on earth. Your life with Jesus will have trials, and maybe even more intense ones than if you were apart from Jesus, but in the end, they will be for your ultimate good.

The important part is believing in God's plan and having faith that the truths we find in His word hold weight, which is why we are called to dig, seek, and see God in His word, in creation, in history, in everything! What really helps remind me of this truth, that His plan is for our good, is when I reflect on how God has been incredibly faithful in my past and I can see where He showed up, even when I was blind in the moment.

They say hindsight is 20/20 and though it is tough having that initial faith to believe in God's plans for you, what a joy it is to reflect and point to Jesus in those moments in your past and see how He used them for your good and His glory. But you don't have to wait for hindsight.

I implore you to be watchful of God's plan right now! He is working right at this very moment in your life and in mine. Don't wait for it to be the past. Intentionally look for His plan today. It may not look exactly like you want it to, but it will be exactly the way it was intended. And the promise we can cling to is that beyond any doubt, God's plan for our lives is for our long term good. God is good and His plan for your life is good, and this good God is worthy of all our worship.

Chapter 2 - Songs

So Will I (100 Billion X), by: Hillsong Worship, TAYA

King of My Heart, by: Bethel Music, Steffany Gretzinger

Holy Ground, by: Passion, Melodie Malone

No One Beside, by: Elevation Worship

Chapter 3

How's Your Heart?

"Are you still sitting on the throne?"

During my college years, I was part of a ministry called Echo and one year, they had announced they were planning a mission trip to Guatemala over spring break.

At this point I had never felt "called" to go on a mission trip before, but God was really tugging on my heart to go on the trip. I talked about it with my mentor and prayed about it for a few weeks and concluded to go. I had always heard that a mission trip would change your life by opening up your perspective and softening your heart... it really did. In that stage of my walk with God, my heart's bent desires and passions were to make myself the best version of me I could be. That was my priority and, as I mentioned before, I was enrolled in the business school, which greatly supported that self promoting mindset.

I wanted to build my own business, I wanted to achieve my goals, and I wanted to set myself up for success. None of those things are bad things in and of themselves, but the dangerous root that can stem from these is pride, the desire to put myself and my own wants first, and God's Word leaves no grey area on this subject. God directly calls me to humble my heart and put others before myself and my own desires. Although I wasn't stepping on people's heads to boost myself higher, I was definitely not living under Philippians 2.

> "Do nothing out of selfish ambition or vain conceit. Rather, in humility value others above yourselves, not looking to your own interests but each of you to the interests of the others."
> Philippians 2:3-4

How could I live out this verse with a heart for business and innovation? In the business school, selfish ambition is encouraged and almost viewed as admirable, and I thrived in the competitive environment.

During this time, I had been really interested in the new technology of 3D printing and had bought a 3D printer of my own. I was looking at how the innovation would create new business opportunities in the US. This technology could extrude material in a three-dimensional pattern to build items layer by layer with incredible precision and almost no waste. I had brainstormed and researched what this tech could be capable of and wandered into the realm of construction. I had found a machine manufacturer in Russia that utilized 3D printing technology to extrude cement filament and construct actual houses! Like life sized homes!

With a small team in the business school, I revolved an entire class project around a business plan of building the foundational walls of cement structure on the south-east coast of America, and within the tornado valley area, to produce lower-cost cement homes with higher structural integrity and higher margin. The business plan was fleshed out pretty thoroughly, and we had quite a lot of evidence showing what potential a business like this could have. We even reached out to various manufacturers and suppliers to get exact pricing on machine cost, material, transportation and labor, along with all the legal or requirements we would need to get a proper business going.

We had come up with the name "Layer X Construction" and filed our articles of incorporation in Georgia. Everything was set for us to get our first machine to the US along with a small plot of land for testing and storage, if we could get funding, of course. My plan for success was coming together nicely!

Before I knew it, spring break was here and it was time to go on my first mission trip. My bags were packed and we hopped on a plane to Central America. I didn't know it then, but being plucked right out of my selfishly ambitious environment, God was giving me a moment to stop what I was doing, slow down, and to see Him. I was not sure what to expect on the mission trip, but I wanted to go with the mindset of a servant and help however I could, so that's what I did. And it wasn't long before we found out exactly what we would be doing. Can you guess what it was? ...pouring cement.

We were informed that there was a small village in Panajachel, Guatemala that we would help serve alongside the local ministry there, Redeemer's House International (now called Orphan Prevention Community). The village had a large population of orphans and children that many abandoned mothers were struggling to raise, so RHI stepped in to be the hands and feet of Jesus while getting to share scripture with them. They were building a small kitchen that the local kids would come and get food from while hearing a message from the Bible a few times a week. Our job was to lay the concrete foundation and help construct some of the initial cement block walling.

Just a few days prior, my mind was focused on capitalism and financial forecasts on how to build my successful business. Now, God was leading me to see more important matters of His people. He was laying a stronger foundation in my life by putting me on my hands and knees to lay a physical cement foundation for others.

> "And do not forget to do good and to share with others, for with such sacrifices God is pleased."
> Hebrews 13:16

God was teaching me to make my life matter. He was showing me with my own two eyes what was going on outside of my world, outside of the little bubble that was revolving around me. Jesus was waking me up to do something about the areas of my life that were skewed in my heart.

I am not sure if you have ever laid concrete, but it is a tough job, especially in a third world country. There was no cement truck available to mix and pour out the material, there was no jack hammer to bust up and level the ground, definitely no 3D printer to extrude the cement with ease and precision. All we had were shovels, a pickaxe, and some willing hands to serve.

Over the next week and a half, I learned a lot about myself while helping build that little concrete kitchen, and I love how God used that moment to rip out my heart of stone and give me a heart of flesh. He was killing the gross selfishness inside of me that I was feeding, not by reprimanding me, but by giving me a glimpse of a greater purpose. A purpose beyond myself, something even beyond the people we were serving. He was showing me what it means to serve others and the fullness of life we get to experience when we take ourselves off the throne of our lives and humbly give Jesus His rightful spot upon it.

> "I will sprinkle clean water on you, and you shall be clean from all your uncleannesses, and from all your idols I will cleanse you. And I will give you a new heart, and a new spirit I will put within you. And I will remove the heart of stone from your flesh and give you a heart of flesh. And I will put my Spirit within you, and cause you to walk in my statutes and be careful to obey my rules."
> Ezekiel 36:25–27 ESV

Ultimately, our main goal during the trip was to help the community by being the hands and feet of Jesus so they may have a clearer picture of God's love for them and grow closer to Jesus, but it is funny how when we extend our hand out to help others, how much it ends up healing our own heart in the process as well.

That's how God designed it! On the flip side, seeing the hurt in our world, or the needs of your friend or brother, and reclusing into our own selfishness and safety has detrimental cost.

> "But if anyone has the world's goods and sees his brother in need, yet closes his heart against him, how does God's love abide in him? Little children, let us not love in word or talk but in deed and in truth."
> 1 John 3:17-18 ESV

We miss out on the opportunity to abide in God's love. To be His loving hands and feet to others. And even beyond that, we miss out on serving Him directly. God says that whatever you do for others, you do for Him. So why wouldn't we jump at the privilege of leveraging our lives to serve a loving King?

> "And the King will answer them, 'Truly, I say to you, as you did it to one of the least of these my brothers, you did it to me.'"
> Matthew 25:40 ESV

One of my friends, who was also on the Guatemala trip, liked to ask people this question: **"How's your heart?"**

The first time I heard her ask that question, I was a bit taken back admittedly. What a forward, personable, and real question! It doesn't have the same vague greeting tone that you interpret when someone, just from habit or social anxiety, asks "how's it going?" Or "hey, what's up?" The question "how's your heart?" immediately goes deeper and shows you that another person actually cares to hear your response and discuss with you what has actually been stirring in your soul underneath the surface. I'm serious, today ask someone you care about, "how's your heart," and see what kind of response you get.

Jesus is always asking us "how's your heart?" and we could have those life giving discussions with Him, if we would just make time to listen to Him. God has a lot to say about the heart and He wants us to recognize when it is broken and bent so He can bring healing and alignment to it. The heart is powerful and can lead to a lot of life, or a lot of destruction. In God's Word, we see time and time again our human heart's true colors when separated from Jesus. In Jeremiah, he states:

> "The heart is deceitful above all things and beyond cure. Who can understand it?"
> Jeremiah 17:9

Jesus knows this, and that's why He is in the business of healing, because He is the only one who can. When aligned with Jesus, the heart is beautiful. Apart from Jesus, the heart is deceitful, beyond any human cure. It is not up to you to cure your heart, because Jesus is the only one who can and has already made a way for healing. When aligned with Jesus, from the heart flows love because our Lord is love Himself, and sent His son Jesus so we could find love and life in Him.

> "For God so loved the world that he gave his one and only Son, that whoever believes in him shall not perish but have eternal life. For God did not send his Son into the world to condemn the world, but to save the world through him."
> John 3:16-17

Do you see why it is so important to recognize who, or what, is on the throne of your heart? When it is you or I on the throne, it only leads to destruction, but with Jesus directing us, our heart can be healed and restored! Step off of the throne of your heart today if you see yourself still at the center of your world, and let the good King of creation be the captain of your life. So… "How's your heart?"

There is much more I could add to talk about the heart, but I want the plentiful scripture on the heart to have the loudest voice. You will need to do some Bible digging to get the full context of these verses, but see the next pages for some starting points you can use to see what God's word has to say about the heart.

After you read through these verses, pick a few that stand out to you, put on some instrumental worship music, and open up to those verses in your Bible. As you read the surrounding context, see the truths of goodness that come to a heart enthroned by Jesus.

Chapter 3 - Songs

Have My Heart (Vamp), by: Elevation Worship

Who You Say I Am, by: Hillsong Worship, Reuben Morgan

Here's My Heart, by: Passion, Crowder

Oh How I Love You, by: Jesus Culture, Chris Quilala

Love Note, by: UPPERROOM, Abbie Gamboa

Heart Verses

"Trust in the LORD with all your heart and lean not on your own understanding: in all your ways submit to him, and he will make your paths straight."
Proverbs 3:5-6

"Create in me a pure heart, O God, and renew a steadfast spirit within me"
Psalm 51:10

"Above all else, guard your heart, for everything you do flows from it."
Proverbs 4:23

"My flesh and my heart may fail, but God is the strength of my heart and my portion forever."
Psalm 73:26

"And the peace of God, which transcends all understanding, will guard your hearts and your minds in Christ Jesus."
Philippians 4:7

"Peace I leave with you; my peace I give you. I do not give to you as the world gives. Do not let your hearts be troubled and do not be afraid."
John 14:27

"Take delight in the Lord, and he will give you the desires of your heart."
Psalm 37:4

"I will give thanks to you, Lord, with all my heart; I will tell of all your wonderful deeds."
Psalm 9:1

"Test me, Lord, and try me, examine my heart and my mind; for I have always been mindful of your unfailing love and have lived in reliance on your faithfulness."
Psalm 26:2-3

"The Lord is close to the brokenhearted and saves those who are crushed in spirit."
Psalm 34:18

"Blessed are the pure in heart, for they will see God."
Matthew 5:8

"For where your treasure is, there your heart will be also."
Matthew 6:21

"The one who has clean hands and a pure heart, who does not trust in an idol or swear by a false god. They will receive blessing from the LORD and vindication from God their Savior. Such is the generation of those who seek him, who seek your face, God of Jacob."
Psalm 24:4-6

"May these words of my mouth and this meditation of my heart be pleasing in your sight, Lord, my Rock and my Redeemer."
Psalm 19:14

Chapter 4

Heart On Fire

"Reject the comforts of lukewarmness and be part of a greater story."

> "But we are not of those who shrink back and are destroyed, but of those who have faith and preserve their souls."
> Hebrews 10:39 ESV

I thought it fitting to delve into the topic of passivity directly after the introspection of our own hearts. Largely because of a concern I have with my own heart at times, and the heart of the American church as a whole. The concern that we can read, learn, and grow our minds... but never apply the truths and knowledge we gain.

Even in the 1940s C.S. Lewis has much to point out about the individual temptation of selfishness and how often it can lead to comfort and stagnation in our lives. In his fictional book "The Screwtape Letters," C.S. Lewis writes from the perspective of a respected devil named Screwtape teaching his nephew, Wormwood, how to best tempt and destroy the life of his nephew's human subject. There are many ways we see young Wormwood attempt to lead his human assignment astray. He uses every method of sin he can to tempt the young human from repentance and from deepening his trust in God.

Uncle Screwtape points out to Wormwood that one of the effective ways to derail a human is through a combination of selfish distraction, comfort, and fear that results in the human taking no meaningful action.[1]

This idea of being stuck because of all the distraction, comfort, and fear is something I like to call selfish passivity. I don't necessarily mean passivity in the sense that you aren't doing anything. As we talked about earlier, we all are worshiping something, even if that something looks like sitting on the couch all day getting absorbed by Netflix for hours on end. Binging Netflix is still an active action taken. A decision on how to allocate your time.

We give our time and effort away to what we worship, and selfish passivity is when we dump our energy into whatever

---

1. C.S. Lewis, The Screwtape Letters

catches our attention, excluding the efforts and plans God designed our lives to pour into, leaving us passive in the important mission of Christ and active in our own selfish desires.

It's this reality that the enemy does not have to lead and tempt you into some drastic sinful act to pull you out of the fight for Jesus. All he has to do is distract you from your mission by putting a shiny object, or a never-ending dopamine-driven feed of entertainment, in front of your eyes and allow you to choose to abandon, or forget about, your stake in the story of Christ. God Himself has much to say about this danger, and in this chapter I want us to see Jesus' words in this area by looking at a heart position called lukewarmness.

Lukewarmness

Lukewarmness is the state in which you are neither hot nor cold. You have not chosen to stand on either side of the fence, but sit in the middle, or like a pot of boiling water, the flame underneath it has gone out, bringing its temperature down to meet the temperature of the environment. In Revelations 3 we are brought into a scene where Jesus is speaking to The Church as a whole, and in verse 14 we see Him talking to a specific church in Laodicea which I believe directly applies to the church we live in today.

> [14]"And to the angel of the church in Laodicea write: 'The words of the Amen, the faithful and true witness, the beginning of God's creation.
> [15]"'I know your works: you are neither cold nor hot. Would that you were either cold or hot! [16] So, because you are lukewarm, and neither hot nor cold, I will spit you out of my mouth.
> [17] For you say, I am rich, I have prospered, and I need nothing, not realizing that you are wretched, pitiable, poor, blind, and naked. [18] I counsel you to buy from me gold refined by fire, so that you may be rich, and white garments so that you may clothe yourself and the shame of your nakedness may not be seen, and salve to anoint your eyes, so that you may see.
>
> [19] Those whom I love, I reprove and discipline, so be zealous and repent.
> [20] Behold, I stand at the door and knock. If anyone hears my voice and opens the door, I will come in to him and eat with him, and he

with me. [21] The one who conquers, I will grant him to sit with me on my throne, as I also conquered and sat down with my Father on his throne. [22] He who has an ear, let him hear what the Spirit says to the churches.'"
Revelations 3:14-22 ESV

First, we see Jesus knows the works of the people in the church of Laodicea. But what is His response to their works? He says that they are neither hot nor cold. And in this context, Jesus is speaking to the spirit of those in the church. Jesus is saying that, opposite of a spirit on fire for Jesus, ready and eager to share the message of truth, we see them as having lost their fire and zeal for Christ. In Jeremiah 20:9 we get to see what a spirit on fire looks like. Jeremiah is being persecuted for sharing the truth that God has shared with him, and the surrounding people are trying to make him stop. This is Jeremiah's response to those people.

> "But if I say, 'I will not mention his word or speak anymore in his name,'
> his word is in my heart like a fire, a fire shut up in my bones.

> I am weary of holding it in; indeed, I cannot.
> Jeremiah 20:9

Jeremiah has no choice but to proclaim God's truth because it is like a fire inside his bones that cannot be contained! On the other side, being cold means you have not aligned your allegiance to Christ. Being separated from God is not God's desire, but at least God can work on a cold person's heart toward repentance. A lukewarm individual may have verbally aligned their heart and soul with Jesus, but has abandoned their post, stopped sharing His name with others, and has been distracted from the mission Jesus has for them. This is where the real danger is.

In Matthew 10, Jesus says that as followers of Him that proclaim His name to others, He will speak our names to His Father in heaven on our behalf.

> "So everyone who acknowledges me before men, I also will acknowledge before my Father who is in heaven, but whoever denies me before men, I also will deny before my Father who is in heaven."
> Matthew 10:32-33 ESV

This declaration points to the fact that Jesus will be our advocate in heaven when we die because of our faithfulness to follow Him and share His name with others. When in the judgment seat of God, we deserve eternal separation from Him, but because of Jesus' gracious word and willing sacrifice, we get the best deal of all time, trading eternal death for eternal life. Importantly, we only receive Jesus' gift of salvation if Jesus speaks our name to His Father in heaven.

In Revelations 3:16, we see Jesus is so disgusted by the lukewarmness of the people's actions in the church of Laodicea, that He spits them out of His mouth. He does not speak this person's name to the Father because they are lukewarm, deceiving themselves into thinking they are followers of Jesus. In Matthew 10:32 Jesus says that because we deny Him before others during our time on earth instead of acknowledging Him, He will deny us before His Father in heaven. That is probably the most terrifying verse in all of the Bible.

Now it is important for us to clarify salvation as a Christian and identify what it is, and isn't, because this truly is a sobering piece of scripture, but also a dangerous one if taken the wrong way.

> "For it is by grace you have been saved, through faith—and this is not from yourselves, it is the

> gift of God—not by works, so that no one can boast."
> Ephesians 2:8-9

In Ephesians, we see it is God's grace alone that saves us through faith, and that we can do nothing on our own to obtain salvation because it is a gift. Faith alone saves us, then we get to live out our faith. In the book of James, he goes into detail to drive home the fact that faith without action, or deeds, is dead. James clarifies that deeds are evidence of our faith and we cannot separate the two.

> [14] What good is it, my brothers, if someone says he has faith but does not have works? Can that faith save him? [15] If a brother or sister is poorly clothed and lacking in daily food, [16] and one of you says to them, "Go in peace, be warmed and filled," without giving them the things needed for the body, what good is that? [17] So also faith by itself, if it does not have works, is dead.
>
> [18] But someone will say, "You have faith and I have works." Show me your faith apart from your works, and I will show you my faith by my

works. ¹⁹ You believe that God is one; you do well. Even the demons believe—and shudder! ²⁰ Do you want to be shown, you foolish person, that faith apart from works is useless?
²¹ Was not Abraham our father justified by works when he offered up his son Isaac on the altar? ²² You see that faith was active along with his works, and faith was completed by his works; ²³ and the Scripture was fulfilled that says, "Abraham believed God, and it was counted to him as righteousness"—and he was called a friend of God. ²⁴ You see that a person is justified by works and not by faith alone. ²⁵ And in the same way was not also Rahab the prostitute justified by works when she received the messengers and sent them out by another way? ²⁶ For as the body apart from the spirit is dead, so also faith apart from works is dead.
James 2:14-26 ESV

In these verses, James uses Abraham and Rahab as examples of what true faith looks like. In their stories, God asked them to do extremely difficult and dangerous acts, but out of faith, they did what was asked of them and lived out their faith in the God of Israel. Abraham and Rahab were anything but lukewarm. They were faithful because when they were called to action by God; they responded and took action. We see this clearly in the book of James and woven all throughout scripture.

> "For it is not those who hear the law who are righteous in God's sight, but it is those who obey the law who will be declared righteous."
> Romans 2:13

> "But be doers of the word, and not hearers only, deceiving yourselves."
> James 1:22 ESV

So we see that lukewarmness is not an option for us. Jesus has designed our hearts to be on fire for Him and to live out salvation by grace, through faith. The only response of a heart truly aligned with the Creator of the universe will have fruit and action behind their faith. Jesus liked to use the analogy of a fruit tree, I think because of how simply and clear it portrays His message. In Matthew 7, Jesus is referring to the difference between good, true prophets versus bad, false prophets and how, because of their fruit, you can determine their heart.

> "Likewise, every good tree bears good fruit, but a bad tree bears bad fruit.
> A healthy tree cannot bear bad fruit, nor can a diseased tree bear good fruit."
> Matthew 7:17-18

That makes sense. A tree that is good produces good fruit. A tree that is bad produces bad fruit. This is what it looks like to be hot, a good tree, or cold, a bad tree. An advocate for truth with good fruit, or a person of twisted truth with bad fruit. But what if a tree produces no fruit? Let's look at the next verses:

> "Every tree that does not bear good fruit is cut down and thrown into the fire.
> Thus you will recognize them by their fruits."
> Matthew 7:19-20

Again, said plainly. If a tree doesn't produce good fruit, that being bad fruit or no fruit, it is thrown into the fire. If we are lukewarm, we are spat out of Jesus' mouth, we are thrown into the fire. There are so many parallels you can make to this but the important takeaway is that a life truly submitted to Jesus in faith, always leads us to action in the form of fruit, even though it is not the fruit that makes us right before God. This is our worship, our out-pour and fruitful actions rooted in Jesus' love and authority.

Now I want to shift back a bit and ask this question again: "Why is it so easy for us to fall onto the sidelines of our heavenly mission?" In the 21st century, I believe it is largely because we are so distracted that we can't see our true, God given mission, past the worldly blinders that have been strapped to our skulls, and that we have made it so difficult on ourselves to hear God's voice through all the noisiness of life that impacts us daily.

But say we are diligent about listening to the voice of God, spending time with Him, and we can easily see God moving and working in the world around us. We often have another vice keeping us out of the fight. A vice called comfort. In reality, most Americans are either comfortable or are striving for additional comfort. This is usually in a materialistic sense, but can also relate to our fulfillment and gratification.

Materially, the majority of Americans are not familiar with being in genuine need. We confuse our wants with needs often, but rarely have unmet needs for survival. We usually have our material needs met, being clothes to wear, a roof to sleep under, and food to eat. Beyond that, we probably have many toys and devices to keep us entertained and beyond that, careers and cars and massive houses we are striving to acquire to further close the fictional gap between where we are now and the comfortable utopia we have made up in our minds. Or if you are comfortable with what you have, it is not a striving for more that consumes you, but a fear of losing it all.

Material possession and goals are not bad, but they can become stumbling blocks in our faith, which is why they need to be held with open hands. And yes, I know that can be really terrifying. But during Jesus' ministry, He did not have even a humble house to sleep in, a car to get from city to city, or an iPhone to communicate His messages. He had a faith and a mission, that is what is important.

Living with our hands open may very well mean we lose some things, but it also means we are in a posture to receive what God has for us. And often, the gift Jesus has for us is a burning fire in our hearts that turns up the heat on our lukewarm souls and brings us to action for Jesus' mission as God includes our lives in the incredible story of worship that He is writing through creation.

In Europe, when someone accepts Jesus into their heart, they call it being "switched on," like a light switch. It's time to flip the "on" switch of our hearts and be a light to the world. So I urge you, as I urge myself, to ask God to search your heart and reveal where you need healing [Psalm 139]. I also urge you to search and test your own heart yourself so that you may identify your own lukewarmness, if it's present.

"Examine yourselves to see whether you are in the faith; test yourselves. Do you not realize that Christ Jesus is in you—unless, of course, you fail the test?"
2 Corinthians 13:5

How do you examine your hearts? First and foremost, continually make sure Jesus is still on the throne of your life, that He is your true worship. Second, see what fruit the actions of your life are producing. If there is no fruit, strip away the distraction, comfort, and fear (which we will soon dive deeper into) and get off the sidelines.

Step into the fight. Hop off the fence. Say "no" to the multitude of voices and distractions vying for your attention that oppose God's words. Reject the scheming voice of the enemy that says "come on in" to the lukewarm dirty bath water of selfishness and idolization of material comfort. Run into the red hot, fierce battle of life like Jesus did with humility and zeal! Be part of the story that is unfolding every day before our eyes as Jesus is extending His glory to the entire world!

When you complete this chapter, think, search, and uncover your heart posture. We are in the midst of a battle, and as soldiers for Christ, we need to check ourselves regularly. Check that our allegiance is pure and unwavering so that we are fit for battle. We don't have to be the strongest or most put-together person to please God. We just need to be aligned with Jesus and fervent to share His name with others that don't know Him yet out of loving submission to His authority.

I want my heart and life to prioritize that mission more and more every day because I know I can always grow in zeal and be more on fire for Jesus. I have to constantly remind myself of what is ultimate and choose Jesus every day to make that happen, and since you are still reading this book, I assume that is your desire too! So let's gear up and keep marching forward in our purpose with the Commander of creation, Jesus.

> "Search me, O God, and know my heart! Try me and know my thoughts!
> And see if there be any grievous way in me, and lead me in the way everlasting!"
> Psalm 139:23-24

Chapter 4 - Songs

Another in the Fire, by: Hillsong UNITED, Chris Davenport

Breakthrough, by: Red Rocks Worship

Way Maker, by: Leeland

Heart on Fire, by: Citipointe Live

The Man In The Arena

"It is not the critic who counts; not the man who points out how the strong man stumbles, or where the doer of deeds could have done them better. The credit belongs to the man who is actually in the arena, whose face is marred by dust and sweat and blood; who strives valiantly; who errs, who comes short again and again, because there is no effort without error and shortcoming; but who does actually strive to do the deeds; who knows great enthusiasms, the great devotions; who spends himself in a worthy cause; who at the best knows in the end the triumph of high achievement, and who at the worst, if he fails, at least fails while daring greatly, so that his place shall never be with those cold and timid souls who neither know victory nor defeat."

- **Theodore Roosevelt**

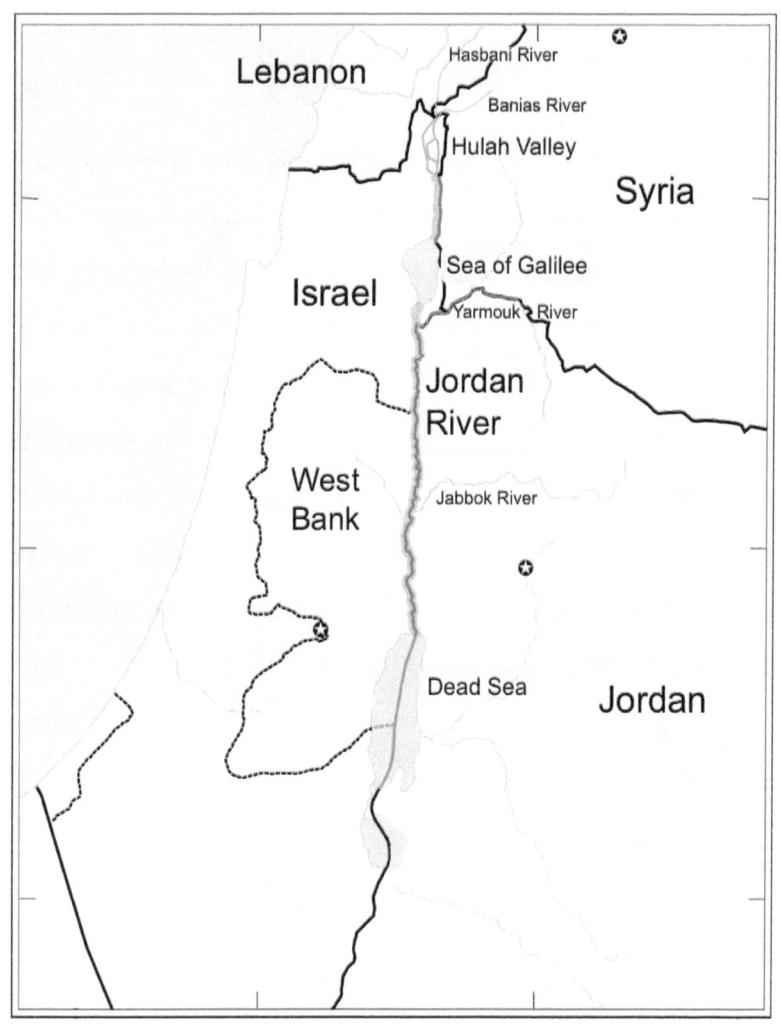

Chapter 5

Life Poured Out

"Stagnation will kill you."

One of my favorite illustrations that symbolizes a flourishing life with Jesus versus a selfish life of "me" is portrayed simply with 2 bodies of water and a river called the Jordan River. This Jordan River starts at a mountain range in Damascus, North-East of Jerusalem, and flows south into two prominent seas. The Jordan River is also where Jesus was baptized by John the Baptist in Matthew 3:13-17 and is an overall special geographic location in the Bible.

As the Jordan River flows southbound, it is a source of nutrients and life for all the people, plants, and animals around it, and eventually it flows into its first large body of water, the Sea of Galilee. This sea is referenced multiple times in the Bible, particularly in the Gospels where Jesus was teaching and displaying miracles such as walking on water or when Jesus commanded Simon Peter to cast his fishing net one last time after a long trip of catching no fish. At the command of Jesus, Simon Peter obeyed and cast his net one more time and he caught a ridiculously abnormal amount of fish that almost sank his boat! For our illustration, the fact is that the Sea of Galilee helps produce an abundance of life and is an important water source for the surrounding area. But after the Sea of Galilee, the Jordan River continues south until it reaches its next large body of water, the Dead Sea.

Contrary to the Sea of Galilee, helping produce flourishing life, the Dead Sea is just that... dead. Though it's beautiful to look at, it is filled with salt and bacteria. No animals inhabit it or fruitful plants spring from it, and beyond hopping in the water for a few minutes to exfoliate your skin or harvesting its salt, it is not great for much else. It smells of rotten eggs, and if you do decide to jump in, it begins to sap the water from your body, quickly leading to dehydration. It's even recommended to keep your swims below 20 minutes to not throw off your electrolytes and hydration level. May I remind you that your body is roughly 60% water, and that the Dead Sea will only suck that precious H2O from your pores.

Bottom line, the Dead Sea does not produce life, but do you know why? Why does the Jordan River, a source of life, flow into and supply the Sea of Galilee, which has lots of life in and around it, then get to this point and suddenly turn sour? It's not because of a faulty source.

The Dead Sea is dead because it doesn't have an outlet. It has nowhere for it to pour out.

This sea just keeps getting filled up from the Jordan River. And without a place for the water to go, the water has nothing to do but slowly evaporate, leaving behind just salt and bacteria. That is also why, if you have ever been camping or hiking, you never drink from stagnant water. You find running water that is moving. That is the water that will be the safest and cleanest to drink from.

What an incredible image of how we are designed to live our lives. Yes, it is important to be filled yourself, but a life of constant filling up and no pouring out will not produce life. An even better solution is to not just pour out, but allow the vessel of your soul to be so filled with Jesus that it overflows with love to the people around you. The only way that will happen is by spending time with Jesus.

Make time to spend with Jesus to be filled and to overflow, because it is in the outflow, the outpouring of our lives, where life and fruit flourish inside and outside of us. As Christians, we have a Father in Heaven that is always willing to spend time with you and I every single day, and when we are intentional about consistently living in relationship with Jesus, we have no other option but to receive the love He has so graciously given us, and pour that love out onto and into others. It's then that we get to truly become a light to the people in our lives. We become a light that can lead others to the source of life that is pouring into our lives, Jesus.

> "You are the light of the world. A town built on a hill cannot be hidden. Neither do people light a lamp and put it under a bowl. Instead they put it on its stand, and it gives light to everyone in the house.
> In the same way, let your light shine before others, that they may see your good deeds and glorify your Father in heaven."
> Matthew 5:14-16

So the real question is, how are you pouring out? If you are pouring yourself out in love, you know the life and love that it produces. Yes it may sometimes bring difficulty, but it ultimately gives life to you and those around you. Now I do want to take a minute to resurface the truth that we are not saved by what we do. We are saved only by the grace of Jesus through faith in Him. But we also see that a life rooted in Jesus has no other option than to pour out.

To follow Jesus is to connect your life to an unending source of life and love. To reiterate, pouring ourselves out is a natural response to Jesus' love for you and I because we should be overflowing! But one may ask, "What if I am not overflowing or pouring out Jesus' love to others? What if I am dry or stagnant?"

I have definitely been in times of stagnation and am familiar with the gross lethargic feeling that comes from my life looking more like the Dead Sea than the Sea of Galilee. Usually it stems from me not taking the time to fuel up by spending time with Jesus. I end up allowing my time to waste away as my own selfish ambitions begin to snowball into the idol of my life. Other times I truly just don't know where and how to pour out.

Fortunately for us, Jesus tells us exactly how and where to look during a discussion He had with a teacher of the law during His time on earth. In Mark 12 we get to hear Jesus talk on the greatest commandments we are to live by. These two perfect commandments cannot be separated, and together they emphasize the importance of the heart and the way we love. The first commandment is directed at our worship, and the second commandment displays the result of our worship. Let's take a look at the passage in scripture:

The Greatest Commandment

One of the teachers of the law came and heard them debating. Noticing that Jesus had given them a good answer, he asked him, "Of all the commandments, which is the most important? The most important one," answered Jesus, "is this: 'Hear, O Israel: The Lord our God, the Lord is one. Love the Lord your God with all your heart and with all your soul and with all your mind and with all your strength.' The second is this: 'Love your neighbor as yourself.' There is no commandment greater than these."
Mark 12:28-31

When asked what the greatest commandment is, Jesus replied it is to love the Lord your God with all your heart, soul, mind, and strength! It is a call to have a heart of worship towards God. A call to live a life revolved around your love for the Creator of life. Then the second command is to allow your heart of worship to pour out to those around you in love. To "Love your neighbor as yourself." The response of having a source of life deeply rooted in the center of our souls is to love. So what does outpouring look like? It looks like love.

Putting others before yourself, helping those around you in need, being a loyal, trustworthy, and honest friend. Being a loving neighbor. That is how to start, and just like selfishness can easily snowball, so does selfLESSness. Jesus' life example gives us some great examples of how this tangibly looks, but here we see He does not give us a rigid list of "to dos." He simply points us to the source of life, then reminds us that the result of being connected to the source of life is love.

From there, He gives us the opportunity and command to act upon His words, to pour out love to the people around us. To pour into our communities, to pour into our neighborhoods, and to pour into the incredibly designed but perfectly broken people that God Himself has hand crafted and put on our path (yes, even the people we may not like or are our enemies).

Take some time to think about the people you can love around you. Are you allowing Jesus to use your life to pour out into the people He has placed in your life? Are you staying connected to Jesus, the source of life and love? Does your life look more like the Sea of Galilee or the Dead Sea?

Whatever the answer, don't let it overwhelm you with guilt. The point is not to instill condemnation, but to make room for conviction to lead us to take action.

Answering these questions honestly gives us a gauge of where we are now so we can further alter the direction we are headed, if needed. When you are ready, let's keep going and look at a few ways we get to pour our lives out to those around us and what the overflow of Jesus can look like.

Chapter 5 - Songs

Oceans (Where Feet May Fail), by: Hillsong UNITED, TAYA

Reckless Love, by: Cory Asbury

Available, by: Elevation Worship

Fresh Outpouring, by: Kim Walker-Smith

Chapter 6

Overflow

"Disciples make disciples."

Jesus being on the throne of our heart leads to an overflow of love, and before I go much further I want to point out the different types of love we see in the Bible (originally written in the Hebrew and Greek language) so there is no perversion of my point when talking about love. In Greek, there are 4 different words for our English word "love" and they all have different meanings. I won't go into full depth, so if you want more details about each type you should read C.S. Lewis' book "The Four Loves." But for our purposes, the four types of love are:

Storge - Affection or fondness for someone or something.
Eros - Romantic or sexual love.
Philia - Friendship and camaraderie.

Agape - Selfless, unconditional, perfect love given to us from God. How Jesus loves us and how we are to love Him and His people.

In most cases when talking about love, I am referring to "agape" love. Love that is unconditional and only a result of Jesus' Spirit living in our hearts and lives, which leads to full freedom in Jesus.

> "You, my brothers and sisters, were called to be free. But do not use your freedom to indulge the flesh; rather, serve one another humbly in love. For the entire law is fulfilled in keeping this one command: 'Love your neighbor as yourself.'"
> Galatians 5:13-14

This is the kind of love we want to overflow with to our neighbor, an "agape" love. This agape love is the word used as the first, and greatest, fruit of the spirit. The fruit that grows from our lives when our spirit is connected to Jesus and walking in line with the Holy Spirit.

> "But the fruit of the Spirit is love, joy, peace, forbearance, kindness, goodness, faith-

fulness, gentleness and self-control. Against such things there is no law. Those who belong to Christ Jesus have crucified the flesh with its passions and desires. Since we live by the Spirit, let us keep in step with the Spirit.
Galatians 5:22-25

If you are a follower of Christ, let's be people that are in tune with and walk with the Spirit inside of us, connected with our Lord and Savior, Jesus. That is the only way we will ever be able to show agape love to those around us. It may look slightly different in various contexts, but the unconditional love that Jesus showed us when He died on the cross for our sin is the love we should reflect when loving others. So how can we show this kind of love to people in our lives? Here are a few ways.

Community

"Beloved, if God so loved us, we also ought to love one another."
1 John 4:11 ESV

Simply put, God designed us to live in community and fellowship with one another. This fact is integrated into our basic architecture. There are many times when God needs us alone so we can have 1-on-1 time with Him, but for everyday life, God built us to have a community around us. He made it this way so we have a web of people around us to both pour into and be filled up by.

To be encouraged by and to encourage.

> "And we urge you, brothers and sisters, warn those who are idle and disruptive, encourage the disheartened, help the weak, be patient with everyone."
> 1 Thessalonians 5:14

To be sharpened by, and to sharpen.

> "As iron sharpens iron, so one person sharpens another."
> Proverbs 27:17

To be lifted up by when we have fallen, and to lift others up when they need help.

> "Two are better than one, because they have a good return for their labor:
> If either of them falls down, one can help the other up. But pity anyone who falls and has no one to help them up.
> Also, if two lie down together, they will keep warm. But how can one keep warm alone?
> Though one may be overpowered, two can defend themselves. A cord of three strands is not quickly broken."
> Ecclesiastes 4:9-12

When we are part of a community, we open up the opportunity to be strengthened by God through His people. We have people we can work through our questions and burdens with. Another huge point is that we can have people around us that care about us enough to love us unconditionally while we are still amid our brokenness, like Christ did. To have a safe place to learn & grow during our spiritual battle here on earth.

> "But God demonstrates his own love for us in this: While we were still sinners, Christ died for us."
> Romans 5:8

Like Proverb 27:17 says, "as iron sharpens iron, so one person sharpens another." We are able to become sharp and to sharpen others when we are honest, open, and intentional about loving others, even in the midst of brokenness and dullness. And how does the enemy begin to dull and break our spirit? Through sin.

Everyone has sin in their life. That is why Jesus had to come. We are called to love the person, and hate the sin. In a loving community, you can bring your sin to the light and allow Jesus to work through His people to fight together against that sin. Sin thrives in the dark, but when sin is brought in to the light, sin begins to die and your heart can heal. Jesus is in the business of killing sin and healing hearts.

In community, we get to experience this breakthrough for ourselves, and we get to help others experience breakthrough for themselves. When we pour out in community, Jesus, through His people, then has room to fill you back up and bring life into your heart so you can again pour out into the people around you.

The people of God are God's Church, and His Church is Jesus' hands and feet to the entire world. God moves through the local church community to impact the broader community, thus impacting the global church. That is why it is vital that we are connected inside the church, and connected with our communities outside of the church.

So far we have been looking at how we can pour into the church community, but we are not meant to stop there. As much as we are called to love each other in the church, we live in a secular and broken world and are called to show love to people outside of the church. We are called to be in the midst of people's lives and communities that don't know Jesus yet so that we can be a light pointing to our source of life.

This is so crucial. We must break from our church bubbles and shells. We are called to be a light for Jesus, to people that do not know Jesus. Then, as we build relationships rooted in love with our communities, we get to extend love to others by inviting them to learn more about who Jesus is. This is the point of our testimony (our story of how Jesus captured our heart). We get to tell people about the fullness of life Jesus has given us as we lay down our lives at His feet.

> "May the God who gives endurance and encouragement give you the same attitude of mind toward each other that Christ Jesus had, so that with one mind and one voice you may glorify the God and Father of our Lord Jesus Christ. Accept one another, then, just as Christ accepted you, in order to bring praise to God."
> Romans 15:5-7

Serving & Sacrifice

We also get to show love in our actions. Whether that is in our work, jobs, hobbies, activities, plans, finances, or general time commitments, we show agape love to people through our lives when we serve and sacrifice in a way that is unconditional and has no strings attached. This agape love from God shows no partiality if it truly has no strings attached. Philia love (friendship love), eros love (romantic love), or storge love (affection) are not bad to have. They are all beautiful types of love we get to experience in our lives, but these loves have a motive, even if it is not a blatantly selfish one.

In contrast, agape love is also known as a charity love. A love that is given away without expecting to receive something in return. A love that has no selfish motive. This is the type of love our servant hearted sacrifices should pour out from.

It is also a love that is meant for the people outside of your current communities. Jesus tells us that when we share that love with others, we are also directly loving Jesus. God delights in our agape love for others, because no matter who they are, that person is a human that God Himself knows and loves deeply, just as He knows and loves you deeply.

> "**35** For I was hungry and you gave me food, I was thirsty and you gave me drink, I was a stranger and you welcomed me, **36** I was naked and you clothed me, I was sick and you visited me, I was in prison and you came to me.' **37** Then the righteous will answer him, saying, 'Lord, when did we see you hungry and feed you, or thirsty and give you drink? **38** And when did we see you a stranger and welcome you, or naked and clothe you? **39** And when did we see you sick or in prison and visit you?' **40** And the King will answer them, 'Truly, I say to you, as you did it to one of the least of these my brothers, you did it to me.'"
> Matthew 25:35-40 ESV

Jesus designed us to serve one another, not to be served. When we humble ourselves and lay down our lives for others, we get to follow in Jesus' footsteps of showing love through service and sacrifice. That is why our heart posture should be in an open position, ready to receive God's love for us so that we may pour out that love through our service and sacrifice.

> "For even the Son of Man did not come to be served, but to serve, and to give his life as a ransom for many."
> Mark 10:45

Discipleship

A mentor of mine gave me some incredible wisdom to always have someone before you, and someone after you. Meaning that you should always have someone in your life that is further than you are on the road you are walking so they may give you wisdom, and someone in your life you are further along than so you may help them navigate the road with wisdom.

This is sound advice for really any road, profession, hobby, or venture, but is especially important in your relationship with Jesus. You need a neighbor that has been following Jesus longer than you have, someone that is ahead of you that can mentor you. Take the position of a learner, a mentee, so you can gain wisdom from their life experiences with Jesus while also creating an opportunity for your mentor to teach and pour out into you.

Second, have someone after you. Remember, life flourishes in the outflow, so have someone you can mentor and pour out into. Being a mentor to someone else fosters life and growth in both your life and your mentee's life. Now it's possible you may think that you aren't suitable or will never be suitable to be a mentor, and I would kindly (with love) encourage you that you are wrong. Yes, maybe having a mentor would benefit you more directly today, but being a mentor is something every person can eventually grow into. No matter where you are on the road, there is always someone who is behind you on the road of faith, and that person could use a loving neighbor.

You may have some mental friction to the commitment to one or both recommendations, but I guarantee you they are both wonderful things to implement into your life. Being a mentee allows you to be humbled while gaining valuable wisdom. Being a mentor, although it can be tough, brings up many growth opportunities for you. It allows you to get more comfortable sharing and teaching others the truths you have found in the Bible, dig into tough questions with your mentee, and pour out love into another human that God designed, created, and loves unconditionally.

"A new command I give you: Love one another. As I have loved you, so you must love one another.

By this everyone will know that you are my disciples, if you love one another."

John 13:34-35

During my early 20s, I got to prominently experience both positions, of being a mentor and mentee. I was plugged into a local college ministry and found one of the greatest mentors I have had in my life that helped me navigate many of the hard questions and hurdles I was facing. Selflessly, my mentor was always willing to talk to me, willing to teach me, and eager to pour into me every single week as I was figuring out what a relationship with Jesus really looks like. After a couple of years of me being mentored, I remember us talking more deeply about the word *discipleship*.

I always thought of a disciple as just the mentee, the one sitting under the sensei. But Jesus pushes the word one step further. Jesus says being a disciple is taking that apprentice position with a humble, open heart, but then going out and teaching others what you have learned. Jesus wants us all as mentors and mentees to take part in making disciples. Meaning, out of love for others, He wants us to also teach people how to teach people about the ways and life of a follower of Christ. He wants us to be mentors and teachers for others so we can point all the way back to the first teacher, Jesus.

> "You have heard me teach things that have been confirmed by many reliable witnesses. Now teach these truths to other trustworthy people who will be able to pass them on to others."
> 2 Timothy 2:2 NLT

After learning this lesson, I soon had the incredible opportunity to be a small group leader for 10 of the most amazing high schoolers I have ever met. Walking through life with those guys was one of the most fun and life giving experiences I have ever had, and although it was sometimes difficult and took energy and time, it was the absolute best investment I could have ever made with my life in that season. I got to see those guys learn and grow during our time together while at the same time growing myself, because often, the benefit of discipleship flows both ways, and the result is a beautiful relationship filled with fruit, life, growth, truth, and love.

Being a disciple is the essence of having a mentor and being a mentor that passes down the teachings of Jesus. Our first mentor and teacher should always be Jesus, so find a mentor that follows Him with their whole heart and has been following Jesus longer than you have. Allow yourself to be a lifelong disciple as you grow in your relationship with Jesus and remember to take time to teach others the truths you have found so far along the path of life that God has set you on.

The outpouring, the overflow, is what agape love is all about and it is lived out through the Holy Spirit. This is the love that pours from our hearts when our life of worship is pointed at Jesus. A love that bears fruit in our communities, in our discipleship, and in our service & sacrifice. This is the same love we get to humbly receive from God when we accept Jesus as the Savior and foundation of our lives. Only God can give this perfect agape love. It is from Him and for Him. It is this overflow of agape love that results from Jesus being the root in our life and the Holy Spirit filling our heart of worship.

"'Whoever believes in me, as Scripture has said, rivers of living water will flow from within them.' By this he meant the Spirit, whom those who believed in him were later to receive. Up to that time the Spirit had not been given, since Jesus had not yet been glorified."
John 7:38-39

Chapter 6 - Songs

The Blessing, by: Elevation Worship, Kari Jobe, Cody Carnes

Highs & Lows, by: Hillsong Young & Free

How He Loves, by: David Crowder Band

Came To My Rescue, by: Hillsong UNITED

Chapter 7

Calloused Hands

"We have work to do."

When someone talks to you about "work," what is your initial response? Take a minute and think about that. What is your gut feeling about work? Is "work" a word that brings up dread and stress? Does your anxiety rise as you think of the pile of tasks you have to get done this week? Or when someone mentions "work" are you excited and passionate? Do you feel you have a mission to accomplish in your work? Do you gain fulfillment in what you do? Is work a good thing to you... or a necessary evil?

As we dove into Genesis at the beginning of this book, we saw God designed us to work, to be fruitful, and to multiply. When God created Adam in the Garden of Eden, God gave Adam work to do. God told Adam to tend to the earth and rule over it and to name all the animals. That was a lot of work to do, so God created Eve, a helper for Adam, in his work. Quick rabbit trail

- there have been lots of adaptive species of animals and creatures over time, so the exact number of species Adam named was probably significantly smaller than today, but here's a fun fact for you.

[1] Currently on earth there are estimated to be 8.7 million different species of living creatures on the planet! Not sure exactly how we came to that conclusion since we have only discovered 1.3 million of them so far, but again, it's an estimate.

What we do know is that we are continually finding more and more new creatures created by God and that there are still many more to find! That means that our work of naming the ever-growing animal kingdom is still far from done, even today. Now, this doesn't mean that we all need to stop what we are currently working on and start helping to fully discover and name every organism and species on the planet, but it highlights two important facts:

1. Work is designed by God
2. There is still work to do.

Back in the garden, we see Adam & Eve faithfully working with joy, tending the garden like they were designed to. But

---

1. www.bbc.com/news/science-environment-14616161

then Adam and Eve were tempted by Satan and introduced sin into humanity because of their disobedience to God. This sin introduced another reality for work which we see in Genesis 3.

> To Adam he said, "Because you listened to your wife and ate fruit from the tree about which I commanded you, 'You must not eat from it,' "Cursed is the ground because of you; through painful toil you will eat food from it all the days of your life. It will produce thorns and thistles for you, and you will eat the plants of the field. By the sweat of your brow you will eat your food until you return to the ground, since from it you were taken; for dust you are and to dust you will return."
> Genesis 3: 17-19

We see that work becomes difficult and laborious for Adam. Because of our sin, we will incur pain and sweat in our work just to eat and survive until the day we die and return to the dust. That significantly throws a possible wrench into the mix of what it means to have joy in your work now that difficulty is presented! But we must not stop doing work. We are still designed for it.

Even God Himself worked! Genesis shows us that in the creation story, God worked for six days to create our universe before resting on the seventh day. And even more remarkably, when God came down from His heavenly throne to live with us as a human named Jesus, in flesh and bone, He continued to work. Jesus' earthly father figure was named Joseph, and he taught Jesus the ways of carpentry. In Mark 6:3 we get a glimpse into Jesus' work life as He is referred to as a carpenter by trade.

> "Isn't this the carpenter? Isn't this Mary's son and the brother of James, Joseph, Judas and Simon?"
> Mark 6:3

If you have ever tried carpentry, it is not an easy job. It is precise, laborious, skillful, creative, and just overall difficult. Like anything, once you develop skills at your job through practice, it will get easier with time, but the reality is that work is naturally hard as a result of sin. Even in this reality, it is still a great joy to get to work every day if you have the right perspective geared towards your work. Importantly, this right perspective requires a heart posture of worship.

As we have discussed, "worship" manifests itself in many ways. In our relationships, in our time, in our finances, and in our work. Work as worship does not mean we all have to be pastors or hold some religious occupation. It means we need to recognize who we work for, no matter your job title. We need to recognize that any job is a means of worship to Jesus. Doesn't matter if you are a carpenter, lawyer, businessman, teacher, pastor, accountant, or barista; you have work to do for the King of creation. Not because Jesus needs anything from you, but because our Creator designed us to work with diligence and integrity so that God may be glorified through our devoted lives. Simply living out that piece of our design brings joy to our Creator.

> "Whatever you do, work at it with all your heart, as working for the Lord, not for human masters, since you know that you will receive an inheritance from the Lord as a reward. It is the Lord Christ you are serving."
> Colossians 3:23-24

Calling All Creators

Back in Genesis 1:26, God makes an incredible remark, saying that man is created in the image of Himself, God. The Creator of the universe made you in His own image, and like our Creator, we create! Creating things is rooted in our image as a reflection of our Creator, and although God is a Creator on a completely different level, being able to speak matter and life into existence, we have an innate ability and often an internal desire to create.

Carpenters, for example, create furniture or build structures by using the skills and resources God gave them. Musicians create music by producing sound waves and organizing them into melodies. A businessman or entrepreneur creates new products and services and brings them into the marketplace. Mothers and fathers multiply by creating a new life, which will then require countless hours of parenting work to raise that kid into their own created purpose. You get the point. We are mini creators made in the image of the Creator.

God also designed and created all of our environments, then released us into the world to work and create. That fact has freedom and calling attached to it based on how God designed you specifically. God uniquely handcrafted you as an individual with a unique passion and personality, and placed you in your mother's womb. Included in that handcrafting are the specific skills and talents that God has given to you to discover, develop, and use for the glory of God.

That brings us to the element of excellence. What has God made YOU excellent at? Notice that I did not ask what job makes the most money. I did not ask what trade seems cutting edge or smart or what occupation is the most comfortable, safe, and stable. I ask what are you excellent at? Jesus has given every person strengths, and purposeful weaknesses, so that we can figure out what He designed us to do with our lives. Our strengths are often what point us towards the "what" of our heart of worship.

On the flip side, God loves using our weaknesses to further glorify Himself in miraculous ways. Like Moses, a man lacking public speaking skills to communicate God's words to His people in the Old Testament. Or the 12 disciples, a group of average guys that were not as theologically knowledgeable as the religious leaders, but said yes to Jesus, and helped spread the gospel to the world. God will use your weaknesses for His glory in His own ways, but for living out your design every day, use the strengths that God has given you as a member of the body of Christ, and say yes to Him when He invites you to use them.

> Moses said to the Lord, "Pardon your servant, Lord. I have never been eloquent, neither in the past nor since you have spoken to your servant. I am slow of speech and tongue."
>
> The Lord said to him, "Who gave human beings their mouths? Who makes them deaf or mute? Who gives them sight or makes them blind? Is it not I, the Lord? Now go; I will help you speak and will teach you what to say."
>
> Exodus 4:10-12

A great example of allowing God into your strengths and weaknesses is the classic story of David and Goliath. Though David was not a big, strong, traditional soldier (his weakness) like Goliath was, he was excellent at slaying large beasts with a sling and a stone. His years of doing what he was excellent at, protecting his flock of sheep out in the fields, allowed him to be used by God in his battle with Goliath.

God was teaching and preparing David out in the pastures. And David's patient and diligent worship to God, being an excellent shepherd, allowed David to strengthen his faith in God and strengthen his current skills. This faith in God gave David the courage and bravery to use the skills God had given him to defeat Goliath. It required both faith and skill for David to be victorious in his battle, even in a time when David was the physically weaker underdog.

Funny enough, David ends up being a phenomenal soldier, king, and leader for the people of God. He was a man that was not paralyzed by fear or his weaknesses, but allowed God into them. In God's hands, weaknesses often end up turning into strengths. For David, God used his weaknesses and God-given strengths to lead armies and change the world.

> "He trains my hands for battle; my arms can bend a bow of bronze.
> You make your saving help my shield, and your right hand sustains me;
> your help has made me great."
> Psalm 18:34-35

God will show up in our weaknesses. It is our obligation to allow God to train our hands so that we may sharpen and use our God given strengths for His glory.

- Where are your strengths and weaknesses?

- What are you excellent at?

- What are some things that you are going to do with the short time you exist on this planet?

The fact is that more often than not, God is not going to speak audibly to you through a burning bush, or send an angel of the Lord to wake you up and hand you your exact mission in a "Mission Impossible" style manilla envelope. Jesus invites us to figure out the "what" together. He has given you truth in His word, a broad calling to share His glory and His name to the people around you, then He gives you the freedom to do that however you can, as long as it aligns with truth and gives glory to God.

This should not be done in isolation. Often, the people that love you and are around you most, witnessing your work and actions, can help you find out the "whats" of your life. The people that love you can help you honestly identify your excellencies, sometimes even more clearly than you can yourself. But most importantly, is that as you take steps of action in your life to discover and hone your gifts, you walk in them with Jesus. You pray about them and allow God to put a confirmation, or an unsettledness, in your spirit about them.

For your weaknesses, give them to the Lord so He may fill them with His power and might as He sees fit. They too can be where Christ shines through your life the brightest.

> "But he said to me, "My grace is sufficient for you, for my power is made perfect in weakness."

Therefore I will boast all the more gladly about my weaknesses, so that Christ's power may rest on me. That is why, for Christ's sake, I delight in weaknesses, in insults, in hardships, in persecutions, in difficulties. For when I am weak, then I am strong."
2 Corinthians 12:9-10

A mentor of mine would often tell me that "The doing often proceeds the knowing" which I was a bit confused at initially. Yes, there are things we can know without doing, by listening to the wisdom and counsel of others, but for the actions outside of morality and more inside the day to day of what we are meant to do with our lives vs what is wasting our time, you often have to take a step yourself.

God can and has given audible exact steps to His people throughout history, but usually it is after you have taken a step of faith with Jesus and consult your community on your actions, that you will receive clarity and confirmation that you are heading in the right direction or need to make an adjustment in direction. Just remember, confirmation doesn't mean easy or barrier free, it's more of a peace. A prayerful peace that transcends understanding, even if painful or difficult initially.

"Rejoice in the Lord always. I will say it again: Rejoice! Let your gentleness be evident to all. The Lord is near. Do not be anxious about anything, but in every situation, by prayer and petition, with thanksgiving, present your requests to God. 7 And the peace of God, which transcends all understanding, will guard your hearts and your minds in Christ Jesus.

Finally, brothers and sisters, whatever is true, whatever is noble, whatever is right, whatever is pure, whatever is lovely, whatever is admirable—if anything is excellent or praiseworthy—think about such things. Whatever you have learned or received or heard from me, or seen in me—put it into practice. And the God of peace will be with you."

Phillippians 4:4-9

The Measure of Success

Here is a comic graphic that I thought portrayed "unique design" clearly.

The comic has a line of various animals lined up in a row including a bird, a monkey, an elephant, a penguin, a dog, a seal, and even a goldfish all looking at this one man. The man is saying to the animals, "For a fair selection, everybody has to take the same exam: climb that tree." And looking at the animal's faces, you can see they all have a "say what?" expression, except for the monkey, of course. He has a wide, teeth showing, smile.

Obviously, there is no way the elephant, nor the penguin, or any of the other animals are going to climb that tree well. And if climbing the tree is what the measure of success is, then all animals but the monkey will fail. Maybe the dog could potentially climb the tree, but he won't be able to do it with excellence. It won't be natural. They would walk away feeling inadequate because they have been given the wrong measure of success for their lives.

Our true measure of success for our time on earth is if we submit our lives and hearts to Jesus as worship, doing what God has designed us to do, or not. That is even true of these animals, although they are designed with more instinct instead of cognizant freewill choices in life. A monkey was designed to climb, so it climbs, the goldfish was designed to swim, so it swims, and in swimming or climbing, those animals glorify the name of Jesus by doing what He designed them to do.

Even the tree has a purpose and design. God made the tree to grow, so it grows and can either become a wonderful home for many creatures while giving off oxygen for humans and mammals to breathe, or it could be cut down and crafted by an excellent carpenter into a big table that may one day have meaningful discussions and meals around it. Or it may be created into a guitar to make beautiful chords and music that allow us to enjoy the sense of sound. Either way, the tree brings God glory by doing what it was designed to do, fulfilling its purpose.

Scripture has many parallels of our purpose compared to trees like noted in chapter 4. When a fruit tree bears bad fruit or no fruit, it is not doing what is was designed to do and is "cut down and thrown into the fire."

Like the animals in the comic, we have strengths and weaknesses. Like the trees, we have been given a purpose that can be seen through our fruit. But for you and I, our Creator has given us so much more than He has given the animals and trees. We have been given dominion over the world to tend and nurture it, to grow and utilize the resources our Creator gave to us so we may, in turn, create things of our own. There are also unique challenges present to humanity that the animals and trees don't encounter.

God has given us so much ability and freedom, we can get stuck in possibility paralysis. Sometimes we can also get stuck comparing our "climbing or swimming skills" to someone else's talents. Yes, there are levels of talent and there will always be someone more talented than you at a skill, but to be excellent in God's eyes is more about the obedience of using your God-given gifts than being better than other humans.

Challenges like these will be present, but we need to know ourselves in Christ so we may know what we have been excellently designed by God to do. We just have to learn what we are designed to create and work on, practice and hone our God given craft or talent, and drop the comparison game. We need to follow the path God has paved for us already. The individual path He designed you and I for before we were even born.

Through prayer, community, truth, action, and introspection of our strengths & weaknesses, we need to figure out the "what" for our work so we don't miss out on the mission God has given distinctly us as individuals. God's Word tells us that "whatever" we do, do it all in the name of the Lord for the Lord. Our work can be anything, as long as our heart posture is positioning our work as worship to Jesus, and is work that we do with excellence to glorify our Creator's name.

> "Let the peace of Christ rule in your hearts, since as members of one body you were called to peace. And be thankful.
> Let the message of Christ dwell among you richly as you teach and admonish one another with all wisdom through psalms, hymns, and songs from the Spirit, singing to God with gratitude in your hearts.
> And whatever you do, whether in word or deed, do it all in the name of the Lord Jesus, giving thanks to God the Father through him."
> Colossians 3:15-17

Now it's time to get to work. Pick up a tool, put on your thinking cap, and take a step. Figure out what you are designed to do by stepping out and asking the Creator for His guidance and direction. He will give it to you. We just need the courage, faith, and heart of worship to act upon it. To climb and swim, to build a table, or craft a melody. Whether you pick up a hammer or a guitar, drop comparison at Jesus feet and find joy living in your design, then let us all be an encouragement for each person in the body of Christ, helping each other do "whatever" with whole-hearted excellence for our Creator.

Don't be afraid of the blood, sweat, and tears that may be on your path. Let's aim to work excellently in our design through practice and dedication. Whether from the rough wood against your hands in your carpentry, or the hours of time your fingers strum and slide against your guitar strings, allow your life, your time, your craft to glorify Jesus through your calloused hands and your tender heart posture of worship.

Chapter 7 - Songs

Build My Life, by: Housefires

Graves Into Gardens, by: Elevation Worship, Brandon Lake

Good Good Father, by: Chris Tomlin

Canvas & Clay, by: Pat Barrett, Ben Smith

Chapter 8

Spirit & Truth

"A new way to be human."

"But the hour is coming, and is now here, when the true worshipers will worship the Father in spirit and truth, for the Father is seeking such people to worship him.
God is spirit, and those who worship him must worship in spirit and truth."
John 4:23-24 ESV

In Greek, the word "gospel" means "good news." The gospels of the Bible comprise the books Matthew, Mark, Luke, and John. These books of good news are accounts of the life of Jesus and His time on earth. They recall His birth, life, death on the cross, and resurrection. Jesus is the image of God and shows us who God is, embodied in flesh, and these four books are staples of the Christian faith as we get to see the story of the promised Savior of humanity come into the world and defeat sin and death.

These books contain the best news we as humans could ever receive and are treasures passed down throughout history! But for a few decades, only three of them had been available. After Jesus walked the earth, died, rose from the dead, and then ascended into heaven, His disciples moved forward with His commands to continue telling about the good news of Jesus to others! Soon after, the first three gospels were compiled.

The first one was the gospel according to Mark (The Book of Mark), then shortly after, the gospels according to Matthew and Luke were written (The Book of Matthew & The Book of Luke). These accounts were fresh on the mind of these disciples and they put pen to paper to account for what happened during Jesus' time on earth. They show us the miracles and stories of Jesus that teach and sharpen us still to this day. When these books were just written, the people of that time got to learn and share this good news with their families and communities and they became known by the people as good news. But there was one gospel still to be written, the gospel according to John (The Book of John).

John was the youngest of the disciples and is estimated to be around 14 years old when he was chosen by Jesus to accompany Him during His time on earth. He got to spend the next few years following Jesus' footsteps, learning from His teachings, witnessing His miracles, and sharing in His everyday life firsthand. After Jesus' ascent into heaven, the remaining disciples all scattered to share the name of Jesus, John included. Matthew, Mark, and Luke wrote their accounts of Jesus' life and John continued to marinate on the truths he learned from Jesus.

Eventually, the mission that Jesus called His disciples to (to spread His name across the world) led them all to persecution, most to the point of death. Matthew, Mark, and Luke had all now been killed as martyrs for the good news of Jesus that they had been sharing. Even James, John's brother, was beheaded with a sword for sharing the gospel, and John lived through it all. He watched his fellow brothers get brutally killed for the sake of making Jesus' name known. Not just one or two of them, all of them.

He lived through the turmoil of the early Church being massacred and the world trying to silence the message of Jesus, but the Church could not be stopped! The Church and the good news of Jesus, the Messiah, roared through the world as the news of Jesus exploded into the nations!

At this point, John has witnessed a lot in his days. He lived with Jesus, suffered extreme persecution for sharing the gospel, watched all of his brothers and fellow disciples die for the spread of the gospel, and lived an entire life dwelling and meditating on the words that Jesus spoke. It was only after all of that, near the end of his life, when John decided it was time for him to write the gospel according to John (The Book of John), to articulate to the nations that did not yet know Jesus, who Jesus was and is, and to fill in any areas of uncertainty the other three gospels may have not focused on as heavily. In John's gospel, we get to see a more poetic version of the good news pointing to many glaring truths of Jesus. Heres two big ones:

1. Jesus is the Messiah that all of Scripture points to.
2. Jesus wants to know you and once you know Him as your Lord and Savior, He makes you a new creation.

I didn't become a Bryan 2.0 when I accepted Jesus as my Lord and Savior, I became a new creation filled with the Holy Spirit. A creation with a new identity, a new purpose, a new mission, a new heart, and a brand new life of fullness.

Jesus defeated sin and death, and you get to live in that reality! A reality that death no longer has a hold on you because you will get to live an eternal life with Jesus, the Victor! John points to this new creation by going back to the original creation of the world. Genesis 1:1 starts the Bible off with the words "In the beginning" which set the stage for the creation story to unfold.[1] The gospel of John starts off the same way:

> "In the beginning was the Word, and the Word was with God, and the Word was God."
> John 1:1

This is not a coincidence. John's gospel then tells of 7 different miracles that Jesus showed His glory through while He was on this earth to further parallel the 7 days of creation. John's central message of "the good news" is this:

In Jesus, you are a new creation!

Because of Jesus, we now have a new way of being human. A way of humanity that can walk in the holiness of God because of the power Jesus instilled in us through the Holy spirit. That is what it means to be a follower of Jesus today, being a new creation that walks in Spirit and truth. Walking out a life that is marked by the holiness of Jesus' Spirit according to the words He spoke, according to the truths of scripture that He left for us.

An important piece of this new creation I need to reiterate is that we walk by the power of the Holy Spirit. This is a

---

1. http://gnbc.org/genesis-john-revelation-parallels/

monumental shift from the way humans operated under the leadership of God during the Noahic, Abrahamic, Mosaic, and Davidic covenants (the covenants before Jesus' covenant, The New Covenant).[2]

In prior covenants, there were laws in place that, if broken, sacrifices were needed to be made to be made right with God. In The New Covenant, Jesus fulfilled the laws in all the other covenants and paid with His own life the penalty for humanity breaking the binding laws of God. Because the price has been paid, we now get to live in the powerful fullness of the Holy Spirit under the authority of Jesus as King.

A Great Responsibility

> "Do you not know that your bodies are temples of the Holy Spirit, who is in you, whom you have received from God? You are not your own; you were bought at a price. Therefore honor God

---

2. https://www.gcu.edu/blog/theology-ministry/theology-thursday-what-are-biblical-covenants

with your bodies."
1 Corinthians 6:19-20

Having the power of the Holy Spirit inside of us is huge! It is God's power inside of us working to break our human nature and empowering us to live in our original design. It is the Holy Spirit inside of us that allows us to stand before the throne of almighty God and not be crushed by His holiness. Our human spirit wouldn't stand a chance, but with Jesus as our Intercessor and His Spirit being inside of us, we get to dwell with God once again, like it initially was in the garden where God dwelt with man.

With the Holy Spirit living inside of us, we also have a responsibility. If you have seen the first Spider-Man movie, when Uncle Ben is consoling newly empowered Peter Parker, Uncle Ben has an iconic line of wisdom to share with Peter, his grandson. He says, "With great power comes great responsibility." Though Uncle Ben's line, written by Stan Lee, and other people before him have coined this phrase, Luke's gospel points to this truth much earlier.

> "From everyone who has been given much, much will be demanded; and from the one who has been entrusted with much, much more will

be asked."
Luke 12:48

The Israelites that lived before Christ yearned for the intervention of God in their personal lives. God moved in powerful ways, as we see in the Old Testament, but when Jesus came onto the scene, it changed everything. God became flesh and dwelt among us as Jesus, and when Jesus was preparing His disciples for the devastation of His crucifixion that was about to happen, He gives them encouragement of a promise we see in John 15. A promise that Jesus would send a Helper from the Father, the Spirit of truth or Holy Spirit, to bear witness about Jesus to all creation. Jesus even says that it will be to our advantage when He leaves because only then will He send this Helper from the Father that will guide us in truth.

> "Nevertheless, I tell you the truth: it is to your advantage that I go away, for if I do not go away, the Helper will not come to you. But if I go, I will send him to you. And when he comes, he will convict the world concerning sin and righteousness and judgment: concerning sin, because they do not believe in me; concerning righteousness, because I go to the Father, and

you will see me no longer; concerning judgment, because the ruler of this world is judged.

I still have many things to say to you, but you cannot bear them now. When the Spirit of truth comes, he will guide you into all the truth, for he will not speak on his own authority, but whatever he hears he will speak, and he will declare to you the things that are to come. He will glorify me, for he will take what is mine and declare it to you. All that the Father has is mine; therefore I said that he will take what is mine and declare it to you."
John 16:7-15 ESV

As believers, we now have the gift of the Holy Spirit that allows us to walk in power and in truth. This gift is not one to be taken lightly, but one that requires great responsibility and surrender to, because our lives are not our own but God's. In Acts, we see spiritual gifts poured out over the Church. Gifts of supernatural wisdom and healing that no man could make happen. Jesus, through His Spirit, is still moving through His people today and allowing the Holy Spirit to play an active role in our lives is key to living in alignment with the mind, will, and vision of God.

In many church congregations, I have found the Holy Spirit is either abused by human motive or ignored out of fear and uncertainty. I urge you to do neither of these, though not a simple task. I am continually learning what it means to live in the Spirit too and do not have all the answers, but I know that this gift from Jesus is not one we should ignore and certainly not abuse. Allow God and His Word to give further insight on how to operate in the Spirit. Throughout many of the New Testament books, particularly John, Acts, Romans, Ephesians and 1st & 2nd Corinthians, we see clarity on how to live in the Spirit. Spend time with Jesus under these scriptures and allow the Spirit to be activated in your life.

> "But you will receive power when the Holy Spirit comes on you; and you will be my witnesses in Jerusalem, and in all Judea and Samaria, and to the ends of the earth."
> Acts 1:8

The Throne Room

A final picture I want to present in this chapter is one of the reality of prayer and worship amid the throne room of Almighty God. Most of scripture is historical in context, meaning it was written about events that happened before you or I were born. But in Revelation, we get to see a glimpse of what is, and what is still to come. Also written by John through the Spirit, Revelation 4 allows us to peek into the throne of heaven. We see the beauty and majesty of God as the chapter magnifies the awe, power, and holiness of God.

Revelation 4
[1] After this I looked, and there before me was a door standing open in heaven. And the voice I had first heard speaking to me like a trumpet said, "Come up here, and I will show you what must take place after this." [2] At once I was in the Spirit, and there before me was a throne in heaven with someone sitting on it. [3] And the one who sat there had the appearance of jasper and ruby. A rainbow that shone like an emerald encircled the throne. [4] Surrounding the throne were twenty-four other thrones, and

seated on them were twenty-four elders. They were dressed in white and had crowns of gold on their heads. [5] From the throne came flashes of lightning, rumblings and peals of thunder. In front of the throne, seven lamps were blazing. These are the seven spirits of God. [6] Also in front of the throne there was what looked like a sea of glass, clear as crystal.

In the center, around the throne, were four living creatures, and they were covered with eyes, in front and in back. [7] The first living creature was like a lion, the second was like an ox, the third had a face like a man, the fourth was like a flying eagle. [8] Each of the four living creatures had six wings and was covered with eyes all around, even under its wings. Day and night they never stop saying:

"'Holy, holy, holy
is the Lord God Almighty,'
who was, and is, and is to come."

[9] Whenever the living creatures give glory, hon-

or and thanks to him who sits on the throne and who lives for ever and ever, [10] the twenty-four elders fall down before him who sits on the throne and worship him who lives for ever and ever. They lay their crowns before the throne and say:

[11] "You are worthy, our Lord and God, to receive glory and honor and power, for you created all things, and by your will they were created and have their being."

I love having this scene in mind while I am before God in prayer and worship. Like the elders at the end of Revelations 4, when I witness the awe of God, what other response could I have other than to fall down and worship Him? By declaring "You are worthy" to God, I get to join the elders in the throne room declaring God's worthiness.

Then in Revelation 5 we see more details on who it is sitting on the throne of God! Spoiler alert, its Jesus, the Lamb that was slain.

Revelation 5

[1] Then I saw in the right hand of him who sat

on the throne a scroll with writing on both sides and sealed with seven seals. ² And I saw a mighty angel proclaiming in a loud voice, "Who is worthy to break the seals and open the scroll?" ³ But no one in heaven or on earth or under the earth could open the scroll or even look inside it. ⁴ I wept and wept because no one was found who was worthy to open the scroll or look inside. ⁵ Then one of the elders said to me, "Do not weep! See, the Lion of the tribe of Judah, the Root of David, has triumphed. He is able to open the scroll and its seven seals.

⁶ Then I saw a Lamb, looking as if it had been slain, standing at the center of the throne, encircled by the four living creatures and the elders. The Lamb had seven horns and seven eyes, which are the seven spirits of God sent out into all the earth. ⁷ He went and took the scroll from the right hand of him who sat on the throne. ⁸ And when he had taken it, the four living creatures and the twenty-four elders fell down before the Lamb. Each one had a harp and they were holding golden bowls full of

incense, which are the prayers of God's people.
⁹ And they sang a new song, saying:

"You are worthy to take the scroll and to open its seals, because you were slain, and with your blood you purchased for God persons from every tribe and language and people and nation.
¹⁰ You have made them to be a kingdom and priests to serve our God, and they will reign on the earth."

¹¹ Then I looked and heard the voice of many angels, numbering thousands upon thousands, and ten thousand times ten thousand. They encircled the throne and the living creatures and the elders. ¹² In a loud voice they were saying:

"Worthy is the Lamb, who was slain, to receive power and wealth and wisdom and strength and honor and glory and praise!"

¹³ Then I heard every creature in heaven and on earth and under the earth and on the sea, and

all that is in them, saying:

> "To him who sits on the throne and to the Lamb be praise and honor and glory and power, for ever and ever!"
>
> [14] The four living creatures said, "Amen," and the elders fell down and worshiped.

We see it is Jesus who is worthy of our praise! There is much beauty in these two chapters, but I want to focus on a piece that involves you and I today, found in verses 8 & 9.

> "...the four living creatures and the twenty-four elders fell down before the Lamb. Each one had a harp and they were holding golden bowls full of incense, which are the prayers of God's people. [9] And they sang a new song..."
> Revelation 5:8-9

Each elder has a harp and a bowl of incense, and the incense in their bowls are the prayers of you and me, God's people! That is incredible to think about that right now, your prayers are in the throne room of heaven as a pleasing aroma to the Creator of heaven and earth, almighty God! King David knew this as a reality for his prayers, and I believe it is why he was such a man of passionate, real, and frequent prayer! Because prayer is powerful and pleasing to God.

> **A Psalm of David.**
> "O Lord, I call upon you; hasten to me! Give ear to my voice when I call to you! Let my prayer be counted as incense before you, and the lifting up of my hands as the evening sacrifice!"
> Psalm 141:1-2 ESV

The angels and the saint in heaven before God are offering our prayers to the King of kings. Wow! I'll reiterate this, so it sinks in. Your sincere prayers are heard by, and are pleasing to, almighty God. Your difficult and messy prayers are heard by, and pleasing to, ever present God. Your faithful and bold prayers are heard by, and pleasing to, the LORD our God.

God wants you, and to commune with you.

> "And another angel came and stood at the altar with a golden censer, and he was given much incense to offer with the prayers of all the saints on the golden altar before the throne, and the smoke of the incense, with the prayers of the saints, rose before God from the hand of

the angel."
Revelation 8:3-4 ESV

Relationship with you is what Jesus purchased with His blood on the cross (see Revelation 5:9) and through prayer and worship, our words to God get to be before the throne of God even now. Your prayer and worship is powerful. Keep the throne room of God and the fragrant incense of your prayers in the forefront of your mind next time you get to spend time in musical worship and see how it focuses you on further declaring the worthiness of Jesus. If you find yourself in a desperate prayer calling out to God, know that your prayer is before His throne before His feet. In all prayer, know that God hears and cares for the prayers of the righteous.

> "The Lord is far from the wicked,
> but he hears the prayer of the righteous."
> Proverbs 15:29

Those that align their lives to God's will are heard by the King, whether it be a cry of sorrow or a declaration of His goodness.

> "I cried out to him with my mouth; his praise was on my tongue.
> If I had cherished sin in my heart, the Lord

would not have listened;
but God has surely listened and has heard my prayer.
Praise be to God, who has not rejected my prayer or withheld his love from me!"
Psalm 66:17-20

Next time you spend time with Jesus, remember this. Your words, your declarations, have power and are presented to King Jesus before His throne. Imagine standing before Him... what would you say? What would you do?

Allow the Spirit inside of you, the Helper, to come alive before King Jesus. Allow the truth of Scripture to be the declarations you can stand on and pray back to God. Live a life of the Spirit, found and rooted in truth, by living in surrender to His will, spending time in His presence and His Word, and taking time in prayer to listen for His voice. Then you can walk in obedience, in Spirit and truth, aligned with the character and will of the Lord. Jesus has given us a new way to be human that contradicts this world. Live in healthy stewardship of the Holy Spirit inside of you and watch the remarkable plans of God unfold in your life as you say yes to His will and His way.

Chapter 8 - Songs

Here Again, by: Elevation Worship

With You, by: Elevation Worship

Spirit Lead Me, by: Influence Music, Michael Ketterer

Your Will, Your Way, by: Bryan & Katie Torwalt

I Can Only Imagine: MercyMe

Chapter 9

Be Not Afraid

"We have no time to bow to fear."

"Have I not commanded you? Be strong and courageous. Do not be afraid; do not be discouraged, for the Lord your God will be with you wherever you go."
Joshua 1:9

In my home, I have a painting of a tiger hanging in my music room. Created by Scott Erickson, this specific tiger has some great artistic symbolism regarding fear. First, the tiger has 2 arrows in its side, wounded from a battle, but he is in a stance ready to continue fighting, an offensive stance. Second, the tiger is blindfolded, and written on the blindfold are the words "Be Not Afraid." [1]

In this chapter, I want to talk about fear and see what Jesus has to say about it. God's Word addresses fear in many ways, but the 2 main points I want to focus on are how wounds and sight play a role in fear.

Wounds

Like the tiger in the painting, everyone has a wound, a past, a thorn, or a metaphorical arrow in their side that has caused or is causing pain. But perspective drastically shifts when you realize your wound could be there for a purpose. I am not saying that the wound didn't result from something horrific or even evil, but it can have a purpose if we choose to recognize it. Even what the enemy meant for evil, God can and will use for your good.

> "And we know that in all things God works for the good of those who love him, who have been

---

1. Scott Erickson, "Be Not Afraid - Tiger"

called according to his purpose."
Romans 8:28

Your wound could be a deep injury that has caused chaos and questions in your mind. The wound may be there as a nugget of wisdom to remind you of something you've learned in the past. Your wound could be there to instill humility and show you that you are only human, not God. Maybe it's there to be the small bit of discomfort it takes to get you out of your comfort zone, humble your pride, and launch you into action. Or maybe it's there to position your heart in empathy and compassion for others in a specific area.

We all have a past, and our wounds can help us relate to each other, but most importantly, our wounds are precisely where Jesus can give us healing. Wounds show us our humanity and often they become our testimony to God's goodness in our lives, even in the darkest and most broken of places.

"He heals the brokenhearted
and binds up their wounds."
Psalm 147:3

Jesus binds up our wounds! Your wound is not there to create fear in your life or hold you back, but it will if you let it. So what is it there for?

Our wounds are there to glorify Jesus in our story, our personal testimony of Jesus. Our wound is the perfect place that shows our human weakness, so God can display His heavenly strength. God is there to be our source of strength when we are weak, to be our healer when we have taken wounds in battle. And Jesus loves to heal His people. It might not be immediate (although sometimes it is), it might not be physical healing (again, although sometimes it is), but when we press into Jesus, we find true healing for our heart and soul allowing us to press forward into the plan God has laid out for us.

His plan is sometimes hard to see through our limited perspective though. I often wish the road of life had a well-lit course to avoid wounds, but usually it doesn't. Sometimes you bump into the walls and get a few bruises, even when you're on the right path.

Sight

"Your word is a lamp for my feet, a light on my path."
Psalm 119:105

We're given a lamp unto our feet so we may see the next step. Nothing more, nothing less. But we are commanded by our Creator to take the next step God has for us. If you have surrendered your life to Christ and know that He is leading and guiding you, but past wounds or current fears are slowing you down or holding you back, I want to encourage you to keep going. I beg you, don't stop walking down the path Christ has for you, even if stopping feels more comfortable than continuing.

Every race worth running has a level of discomfort, and you have one unique race of life to live and no one else can live it for you. Your path may look different from others' paths when it comes to the "what" of your focus and energy, but that is because your path is uniquely designed for you by God Himself. So although you don't have a full Google Maps printout of God's plan and direction for your life, you can always take one step of faith by relying on His Word. Don't take a step away from your God given purpose, step into it.

That being said, it is okay to start fresh if you are on the wrong path. If you have found yourself on a path of destruction and sin, Jesus is always available for you to turn back to. Align your path back with Christ and He will always welcome you home with love and grace, like a lost child returning home to their father.

Sometimes, before we take the next step down the path God has for us, we first need patience, and will have to wait on God's timing, but don't allow that fact to be a copout for your relationship with Jesus to progress. If God has already opened a door for you to step through but you are "patiently waiting" because it is not the door you wanted or envisioned opening, you are not being patient, you are probably stuck in stagnation. God never calls us to be stagnant with our lives, especially when that stagnation is a fruit of fear or comfort. God opposes stagnation because your faith can never thrive in stagnation. Your faith at this very moment is either growing or dying, and stagnation means it's slowly dying.

You can always continue to faithfully press into God during a waiting season by spending time with Him, and I guarantee if you spend time with Jesus, He will put a step on your path or remind you of the one that is already there. It might not be the step you were expecting, which is how it usually seems to play out, because our steps require faith.

Maybe that big step won't be highlighted just yet, but a smaller one, like calling a friend and encouraging them, or inviting your neighbor over for dinner, might be the thing God wants you to be faithfully obedient in today. Press into Jesus and His words in scripture to turn up the volume on His voice in your life and He will give you a step, and when God does highlight that big step, do not let fear cripple you from taking action.

Even when it feels like we are blinded like the tiger in the painting, have faith to press on in the direction Jesus has directed you to go. You can rely on the guidance of the Good Shepherd that already knows the whole path like the back of His hand even when you do not. Remember that God is for your good and take the next step that Jesus has lit up for you, big or small. Release your cling to the worldly comforts that are holding you back. Reject stagnation rooted in fear and walk through the next door God has opened for you, because although it may be difficult, Jesus promises that following His direction will always be worth it.

Follow Jesus and be not afraid.

> "For I am the LORD your God who takes hold of your right hand and says to you, Do not fear; I will help you."
> Isaiah 41:13

"What If?"

When sin tries to entice you or me to give in to our desires, the enemy usually plants a mistrust of God into our hearts through a fear of missing out on something. Whether that something is pleasure, gain, or something rooted in pride, the enemy likes to exploit an unmet desire. The sad thing is that when you give into the sin that promised to meet your desire, you often get a "quick fix" but end up feeling more empty in the long run with an even larger unmet desire.

Contrarily, when you choose the way of Jesus enough times, you begin to see how God is for your good and fulfills your desires in much different ways than sin tries to. When you choose Jesus' way, sinful solutions to shallow desires fade and new desires deep within your spirit emerge. For example:

Desire to increase worldly comfort gets overthrown by the desire to give to those in need.

Desire to get revenge turns into a desire for your enemy to know they are loved by Jesus.

Desire to abuse substances may be a revealed desire to feel fully alive.

Desire for sexual pleasure may be revealed to be a holy desire to be fully loved.

When you say yes to Jesus' way, His goodness will be revealed to you and transform you. Jesus will show you that you are fully loved, give you purpose to live fully alive, increase your generosity towards the people around you, and light a flame in your heart to share the goodness of Jesus with others, plus so much more. Following Jesus' way allows the fruit of the spirit to flourish in your life and mold you into the image of Jesus. Obedience to Jesus' way allows us to open up our hands and release the "what ifs" of sin and receive the gifts only God can give us to meet the desires of our soul.

Now when I start to feel the pull of this world, I recognize that there is something good that God has for me down the path He has called me to. I recognize that if I don't continue down the path the Lord has made for me, and succumb to stagnation, I will always wonder "what if" to the goodness the Lord had for me through His door.

What if I did take that next step with Jesus? Where would it lead? Would it lead me down a difficult story? Probably. Adventure? Most likely. Joy and fullness of life? Definitely! But if I stay where I've been, I will never get to experience it.

If I allow my flesh to succumb to the paralysis of fear or cheap thrills, I know one thing for sure: I won't have lived my one and only life in the fullness of Jesus. I will one day look back on the vapor of my existence and ask, "what if" with a long face and empty eyes. So each day I will take another step out into the mystery with Jesus, and I encourage you to do the same. Because there is a God created purpose in your journey, a reason for your existence. But if you stop, or run away down another easier path, you will miss out on the fullness of Jesus, as so many do.

> "Teach us to number our days, that we may gain a heart of wisdom."
> Psalm 90:12

There's something special required to live with that kind of boldness. It will not be easy to overcome fear that is so apparent that it seems logical, even wise, to bow to it. Fear can be masked as a worldly wisdom, but it deserves no submission. It takes discernment, courage, and strength to identify and overcome this worldly fear. It will require you to choose to take the heavenly, eternal, true wisdom of God to heart and say no to the disguised dictatorship of fear. But again, the strength that is required to overcome this beast does not come from ourselves. It is a strength and boldness that comes from our confidence and faith in our guide, Jesus.

Jesus has been in our shoes before and has already overcome any challenge we may face. He is the ultimate authority over the heavens and the earth (including the enemy), and can bring you through whatever mountain that fear may disguise itself as.

Jesus knows exactly the trail you're on. He knows where the pitfalls are, where the tough terrain is, where that cliff's edge resides, and where the enemy likes to hide. The enemy would love to derail your God given purpose and mission, if he could only distract you and take your gaze off of Jesus or silence Jesus' voice in your life. God knows you can't see the whole path, He designed it that way, but don't let your lack of vision halt your journey, because we have no time to bow to fear.

I want to reiterate Joshua 1:9 which says, "Be strong and courageous. Do not be afraid;" Notice it uses the word 'courageous' to combat fear. Do you know what 'courageous' really means? Here's the Oxford definition:

cou·ra·geous /kə ˈrājəs/ adjective
    1. not deterred by danger or pain; brave.

cour·age /ˈkərij/ noun
    1. the ability to do something that frightens one.

    2. strength in the face of pain or grief.

God has commanded us to take courage, and being courageous means continuing to move forward in the face of fear, not being deterred by the danger that is on our path. Don't miss it! Live with boldness and faith, knowing that God's plan is for your good. Live with confidence and compassion, remembering that even in the difficulties and pain, Jesus is writing a beautiful story in your life and in the lives of those around you.

Live with intentionality, recognizing that we only have a short time on this earth and don't want to waste it. And live fearlessly in the light because you serve a King that has overcome the darkness. You don't need to see the whole path, you just need to take one more step, knowing that Jesus is guiding you on the perfect, difficult, incredible, fulfilling path He handcrafted just for you.

> "I took you from the ends of the earth, from its farthest corners I called you.
> I said, 'You are my servant'; I have chosen you and have not rejected you.
> **So do not fear, for I am with you**; do not be dismayed, for I am your God.
> **I will strengthen you and help you**; I will uphold you with my righteous right hand."
> Isaiah 41:9-10

"Keep your lives free from the love of money and be content with what you have, because God has said,
'Never will I leave you; never will I forsake you.'
So we say with confidence, **'The Lord is my helper; I will not be afraid. What can mere mortals do to me?'** "
Hebrews 13:5-6

"For God gave us a spirit not of fear but of power and love and self-control.
Therefore do not be ashamed of the testimony about our Lord, nor of me his prisoner, **but share in suffering for the gospel by the power of God"**
2 Timothy 1:7-8 ESV

"Even though I walk through the valley of the shadow of death,
I will fear no evil, for you are with me;
your rod and your staff, they comfort me."
Psalm 23:4 ESV

"**Do not be afraid** of those who kill the body but cannot kill the soul. **Rather, be afraid of the One** who can destroy both soul and body in hell."
Matthew 10:28

CONFESSION TO ONE ANOTHER

"Then I acknowledged my sin to you and did not cover up my iniquity. I said, "I will confess my transgressions to the LORD." And you forgave the guilt of my sin."
Psalm 32:5

The last part of fear I want to touch on is confession. The Enemy's easiest win in your life is for you to keep your sin in the dark, where that sin can hold you captive, and where the enemy can introduce more sin, shame, and fear into your everyday life. I know there can be a weird connotation around confession. It can quickly become a religious duty or checkbox if you look at it as only a religious practice. Or in an environment like the one I grew up in, it is important to confess our sins to God, but confession to one another as humans is not as emphasized.

Jesus tells us to confess our sin to God and to one another because confession brings reality to the surface and allows for our repentant heart to find mercy and grace. A mercy and grace that breaks the power, the chains, of sin.

> "Whoever conceals their sins does not prosper, but the one who confesses and renounces them finds mercy."
> Proverbs 28:13

We are completely dead in our sin if Jesus had not taken on the punishment of our sin, so confessing to God is stepping into humility that we may receive mercy. And accepting the gift of forgiveness that Jesus gave to us, at a steep price to Himself, allows us to receive grace.

Personally, I feel private confession to God is the easier of the two types of confession to step into, although in actuality it should be the other way around. Everybody wants forgiveness, but not everyone wants to share their past wrongdoings or current sinful struggles with another person, especially in the church. That's why even in the catholic church you aren't usually even looking face to face with a pope, but sitting in individual booths, where you can still have that safety of some anonymity and distance.

> "Therefore confess your sins to each other and pray for each other so that you may be healed. The prayer of a righteous person is powerful and effective."
> James 5:16

Jesus says to confess our sins to each other and pray for each other that we may be healed. This confession and prayer could be with a leader or pastor, but it doesn't have to be. I primarily see this as an act of the body of Christ - a community driven activity that allows the body of Christ to find healing, primarily through the people that know and love you the most, and can confirm and encourage your repentant heart with truth. It does not have to be a public announcement, just a real confession to another person who you can share your burden with as they can remind you of the forgiveness Jesus has already offered you.

> "If we confess our sins, he is faithful and just and will forgive us our sins and purify us from all unrighteousness."
> 1 John 1:9

Confession to one another simply brings the darkness into the light, and the light will always overcome the darkness! Satan has no power in the light, and as children of God, you are a child of light. It is where your heart is meant to be, but the scary part of the light is that it exposes. That is the point of light, to expose the shadows and to cast out darkness. Jesus reminds us that when we confess our sin, our sin is brought into the light where those that love us can pour into our lives with prayer, encouragement, and support. If you do not have people around you that fully know and fully love you by calling you higher with grace, you need to find them! You need them, and they need you.

Confession creates vulnerability, and vulnerability opens up opportunity for growth and pain. Vulnerability can strengthen relationships and build up the people of the church, but it is also an opportunity for deep pain to be exposed and abused. So please, say yes to the benefit of freedom by confessing your past and current darkness, but do so amid trustworthy people. And if you find yourself on the other end, someone is opening up in confession to you, please use grace and gentleness, doing everything in genuine love so that person may healthily grow and release whatever sinful chains may have been binding them. If Jesus has already shown them forgiveness (which He has), so should we.

Confession is beautiful. It is something Jesus knows we need. We just have to be loving, mature brothers and sisters that will initiate vulnerable confession so that Jesus may work in those areas of our lives. Those discussions and confessions will build trusting, strong relationships that invite others to open up as well, breaking chains of darkness all throughout the church! Be the initiator. Take Jesus at His word and see how confession to God and to one another, backed with fervent prayer, changes the people, the hearts, and the communities in your life.

When confronting fear, the enemy has many tactics to stop you in your tracks. Instead of allowing fear to stop you, overcome fear through faith in the goodness of God. Allow your past wounds and the transformation of your life to be a testament to God's glory. Press forward in your walk with Jesus even when you can only see the next right step because you know you have a Good Shepherd. Leave behind whatever sinful desires your hands are still clinging to and open your palms up to the better gifts of God.

Remember that you are loved and forgiven when you bring your darkness into the light in confession and repentance. Decide today to further break off fear from your life, and live a life of courage following the One who offers abundantly more than what the results of fear could ever offer. Be not afraid, for God is with you wherever you go.

"Have I not commanded you? Be strong and courageous. Do not be afraid; do not be discouraged, for the Lord your God will be with you wherever you go."
Joshua 1:9

Chapter 9 - Songs

Battle Belongs, by: Phil Wickham

No Longer A Slave, by: Bethel Music, Jonathan David Helser, Melissa Helser

Never Lost, by: Elevation Worship

Take Courage, by: Bethel Music, Kristene DiMarco

CHAPTER 10

YOU CALLED MY NAME

"DO YOU KNOW HIS VOICE?"

I was always a bit confused when God was referred to as a "jealous" God, but I can now see what it means. We serve a God that wants, more than anything, for your life to attain its full purpose by glorifying Him. For you to recognize the price Jesus paid for your salvation and to continue to put God as the number one priority in your life above all else, like the apostle Paul did.

> "Indeed, I count everything as loss because of the surpassing worth of knowing Christ Jesus my Lord. For his sake I have suffered the loss of all things and count them as rubbish, in order that I may gain Christ"
> Philippians 3:8 ESV

Our God is righteously jealous toward the worthless rubbish that vies for our attention every day as we waste our precious time on earth distracting ourselves from our God given purposes.

Imagine you just got a new puppy. Now all you want to do is spend time with the puppy, play fetch with him, teach him new things, feed him, and walk with him. You take good care of him and give him plenty of room to run and grow. Now imagine after a couple of years he has grown up a bit, and one day he somehow consciously runs away from you because he felt you did not have his best interest in mind.

Your dog somehow had a thought planted in his mind that you were not what he wanted and that he didn't need you. You gave him food and shelter and all he wanted to do was get as far away from you as possible. And to make things worse, his favorite thing to do is to run out into the street and play chicken with oncoming traffic. That would be heart-wrenching for us. Imagine what almighty God feels when we, His creation and children, do that to Him. We know God is for our good, yet choose to run from Him.

If you are a parent raising a child, I am sure you can relate to this feeling much closer as a mother or father. You may not be perfect, but you always want good for your kids. Now imagine a father that is perfect and is perfectly guiding your life for your good, has the perfect wisdom you need for your situation, and gives you the perfect amount of resources and trials to allow you to grow and flourish. Does that sound like a father you would want to run from, or a father you want to be close with and learn from?

Sheep Need A Shepherd

I love my dog Domino. I picked him up from a local animal shelter 13 years ago when writing this and he has been by my side ever since. Though you may disagree, he indeed is the best dog on the planet. He is obedient and smart, friendly, and will love you no matter what. I have taught him to sit, stay, come, lay down, put his paws up on in arm, and importantly, I have taught him his name, "Domino." A dog foremost needs to know their name, so they know when they're being addressed. It is crucial for them to know their name, so when they are in danger, they know you are addressing them when you say another command like "come," "go," or "stay." But since Domino has gotten older, he has become less obedient, generally because of stubbornness. He is losing a bit of his hearing and doesn't respond quite as well to his name or what I tell him, and it has gotten him into some dicey situations.

Jesus does not call us dogs, but He compares us to sheep, because He knows we need a shepherd. Although sheep are not the smartest or strongest animal in the kingdom, they have some unique attributes. They feel emotion for other sheep, build friendships in their herd, and fight alongside each other if ever needed. Most importantly, their learning and recognition capabilities are strong. When they are given their name, they remember it, and when they have a shepherd they know will protect them, they will easily identify the shepherd's face and voice out of a crowd.

[1] They are social animals that learn and recognize well, but need leadership. Like sheep, we need to know who we are, and we need to recognize the face and voice of our Shepherd.

Another thing about sheep is that they wander. They will just start eating some grass in a pasture, then find another little patch they like a few yards away, then another, until they are far off from the herd and their shepherd. At this point, they are in danger. The sheep now has two options. To keep just doing its own thing and hope a predator doesn't come up and devour them, or to find their shepherd.

---

1. http://www.bbc.com/earth/story/20170418

Sheep unfortunately aren't always able to recognize they are in danger and don't seek out the shepherd. The shepherd then has to find them before they become a lucky predator's dinner. Luckily for us, our shepherd is always calling out for us when we go astray and pursues us when we get turned around. When we are lost, we need to recognize we are in danger and know the voice of our shepherd so we know how to get back to Him. And when the enemy comes to destroy us, which he will, the shepherd pursues us and protects us, even to the point of death.

> "I am the good shepherd. The good shepherd lays down his life for the sheep."
> John 10:11

We have a good shepherd that has laid His life down for us, His sheep. But our shepherd, who overcame death, is alive and well on the throne. He is calling our names to come to Him to this day.

Have you had a personal experience of frustration when you are trying to lead but are not being followed? Whether with your child, friend, partner, dog or possibly even a sheep, it is frustrating when our call is ignored. I can imagine Jesus feels similarly when we do not respond when He calls our name.

When we just keep doing whatever we want to do without allowing Jesus to lead us, we end up hurting ourselves. Sure, we may get temporary pleasure in whatever shiny object distracted us and caught our attention, but ignoring Jesus is a double negative. When we ignore Jesus, we put ourselves in danger and miss the goodness of His calling on our lives. That is why it is crucial for us to recognize God's voice and listen when He calls our names.

The Choice is Yours

"When Jesus saw the crowd around him, he gave orders to cross to the other side of the lake. Then a teacher of the law came to him and said, 'Teacher, I will follow you wherever you go.' Jesus replied, 'Foxes have dens and birds have nests, but the Son of Man has no place to lay his head.' Another disciple said to him, 'Lord, first let me go and bury my father.' But Jesus told him, 'Follow me, and let the dead bury their own dead.' Then he got into the boat and his

disciples followed him."
Matthew 8:18-23

We live in a world where Christianity can be a casual religion, a legalistic lifestyle, or a box that you check on Sunday, but Jesus is not interested in your religious facade or jargon. Jesus wants to know you deeply in relationship and wants to use your life to glorify His name. Jesus knows your name and is calling you through His word to you, but the earthly cost is high to follow Him. Following Jesus is much bigger than just learning about Him on Sundays. Following Jesus is laying your life down in surrender to Him as your one and only Lord and Savior. A surrender that lays down self interest and glorifies the Creator through faithful obedience.

> "Then Jesus said to his disciples, "Whoever wants to be my disciple must deny themselves and take up their cross and follow me."
> Matthew 16:24

Jesus, who was crucified on a cross, is telling His disciples here that following Him will mean taking up their own cross. He calls them to deny their own lives and desires, and to pick up the mission Jesus has for them even if it leads to persecution or death. This is not something Christians today can opt out of.

We have the same mission of proclaiming the gospel of Jesus to the world, and that mission will lead to persecution. All we have is the choice to accept Jesus' invitation or not. Jesus is not in the business of convincing people to follow Him. If anything, His words turn many people away because of the radical cost of obedience. So why did the disciples, and why do Christians today, follow Jesus?

The disciples got to witness Jesus' remarkable power as the Son of God and knew Him to be the Messiah, the promised Savior of Israel. In Matthew 16, Jesus reminded His disciples of it being worth it to follow Him. When He returns to earth, there will be a heavenly reward for whoever follows Him and live out the mission He called them to.

> "For the Son of Man is going to come in his Father's glory with his angels, and then he will reward each person according to what they have done."
> Matthew 16:27

So what is the reward for such a steep cost? On top of getting to live a life of fullness here on earth, the true reward is eternal life with your Creator. It is the opportunity to be face to face with Jesus and live life as God designed it before sin entered the world. It is a reward that outweighs any earthly measure or accolade that we can try to achieve here on this side of heaven. Maybe there is an additional or varying reward on top of that since Jesus did say "according to what they have done," but being in the presence of God is the grandest gift my human brain can comprehend. What I do know is that God is good and gives good gifts, so if He promises eternal reward, I want to invest in it.

Jesus is upfront about the cost and reward of the decision to follow Him or not. Counting the costs, the disciples did decided to follow Jesus' path. That decision led all of them to persecution and nearly all of them to death as they proclaimed the name of Jesus. Following Jesus may not always lead to such extreme persecution, but difficulty is promised along the path Jesus charted for us.

Just like Jesus called the disciples by name to follow Him, He calls you and me to the same mission they had. To share the gospel of Jesus to the world. This includes our local neighborhoods and communities and further extends throughout the entire world to people that have never heard the name of Jesus yet. We are called to use the gifts and talents stewarded to us to shine the light of Jesus. To magnify the One who overcame death and made a way to the Father for us.

Your name has been called by the Father to go. Your life has been commanded by Jesus to share the good news of the gospel with those who have not had the opportunity to hear it yet. Your soul has been filled up by the Holy Spirit to have the strength and power to respond to this call. Now we get to go and make disciples of all the nations!

Will you accept the mission?

> "Go therefore and make disciples of all nations, baptizing them in the name of the Father and of the Son and of the Holy Spirit, teaching them to observe all that I have commanded you. And behold, I am with you always, to the end of the age."
> Matthew 28:19-20 ESV

Whether you are single, married, have kids, are running a business, are up to your eyeballs in responsibility, or a free bird, you are called as a follower of Jesus to make disciples. Kids, businesses, and normal life responsibility are important, so I am not saying to neglect or exclude yourself from those things, but life prioritization is essential to fulfill your purpose in allegiance to Jesus.

Priorities

Life consists of important priorities, unimportant things we can give our time to, and two ultimate priorities. There is always a cost to any yes because we have limited days on earth, and the world does not make it easy to keep the ultimate thing priority in our hearts, minds, and actions.

The first ultimate priority is our relationship with God, to love Him fully. And our second ultimate priority is to love His people, a result and proponent of the first ultimate priority.

> "Teacher, which is the greatest commandment in the Law?" Jesus replied: "'Love the Lord your God with all your **heart** and with all your **soul** and with all your **mind**.' This is the first and greatest commandment. And the second is like it: 'Love your neighbor as yourself.' All the Law and the Prophets hang on these two commandments."
> Matthew 22:36–40

1. Love the Lord your God with...
- All your **heart**: Have a relationship with God by getting to know Jesus. Spend time with Him in prayer and wor-

ship to enjoy His presence. Dwell on His goodness and love for you.

- All your **soul**: Allow the Holy Spirit inside of you to lead your soul by creating space and solitude to hear from the Holy Spirit. God gave us the Holy Spirit to be our Helper on earth till our soul is with Him in eternity. Allow Jesus to fill your desires with what God desires.

- All your **mind**: Let God's words transform your mind by reading scripture. Saturate your mind in His words so that He can show you the world through His ultimate lens on humanity.

"Trust in the LORD with all your heart and lean not on your own understanding; in all your ways submit to him, and he will make your paths straight."
Proverbs 3:5-6

By loving the Lord your God with all your heart, mind, and soul, you will align your heart with the heart of God.

This is also the only way you will be able to effectively live out ultimate priority number 2:

2. Love Your neighbor as yourself.
- Be a light to the people around you and help others to encounter a loving God through your love towards them.

- Grow in zeal and desire to love people that do not know Jesus yet, and take action to get His message to them.

These are the 2 ultimate things that matter most. Keep them top priority.

The things in life that are not ultimate, but are important are the hardest ones to prioritize. Mainly because they are all things we love and care about, but important things can not overshadow ultimate things, no matter how important they are. Family, friends, work, community, side hustles, talents, and hobbies are all important things. This list looks different for everyone, though I observe the most healthy people have people and relationships highest on this list.

Take out a piece of paper and think through your priorities. Write them all out from the highest priority to the lowest. Now here's the challenging part. Choose only 5-10 of them you will keep as important priorities this year. This list can change and be re-ordered, but I recommend limiting this list to what you can healthy prioritize each year with the time you have. This will allow you to steward your yeses well instead of over-committing and doing too many things poorly.

The unimportant things are the easiest to give our time to (Netflix, video games, social media, etc), yet they are the ones that leave us the least fulfilled when we give into their pull. They are not inherently bad in moderation, but can quickly consume our most valuable asset: time. These are also the places we can take the quickest action to reclaim precious hours of our day while combatting the mental strain mass media can put on our well-being. Use whatever discretionary time you have wisely by moderating or eliminating the unimportant things in your routine and you will have an enormous head start on prioritizing your life.

Next, write out your top 3 unimportant time suckers on a piece of paper. Some of these "unimportant priorities" do provide some benefit, like enjoying a show with your spouse or connecting with friends on social media, but I would encourage you to set boundaries around these time suckers by defining limited free time in your day for them. Choose specific windows of time during the week you allow yourself to enjoy in these activities so that the time does not mindlessly slip from your days.

Boundaries will help you not only manage these embellishments from getting out of hand, but will also allow you to enjoy them more when you look forward to your window of free time.

Most importantly, to combat time suckers and be true to your priorities, fall more in love with Jesus by pursuing the missions and people that He is pursuing. Take up the joy of the Lord as you give more than you take. Be filled with gratitude as you serve more than you are served. Find a ministry that resonates with your heart and press into it with your friends and community.

When you live a life of mission, spiritual fruit will spring up in your life. There will be times where your faith in Jesus will have great earthly cost, but will also reap rich reward on heaven and on earth. There is a cost to every yes, and only you can allocate your "yeses" in your own life. Choose wisely, they are limited.

COUNT THE COST... OF NOT FOLLOWING JESUS

Limiting time suckers and keeping important things in proper priority will have a cost, but when we do not allow the ultimate things to be first, the cost is far more grim. Allowing the ultimate priorities to sink to the bottom of our list usually has distraction or pride at the root, and the danger is that we then rely on our own strength, our own heart/soul/mind, to sustain us instead of the love of Jesus. Here are a few specifics:

1. When we rely on our own heart = Fruitfulness begins to die.

When family comes before God, as a result you cannot be the best for your family.

When rules come before God, you become a slave to legalism and lose your joy.

When community and ministry come before Jesus, you start looking like Martha and will soon be burnt out of ministry, instead of Mary who sat at the Lord's feet.

At the Home of Martha and Mary

As Jesus and his disciples were on their way, he came to a village where a woman named Martha opened her home to him. She had a sister called Mary, who sat at the Lord's feet listening to what he said. But Martha was distracted by all the preparations that had to be made. She came to him and asked, "Lord, don't you care that my sister has left me to do the

work by myself? Tell her to help me!" "Martha, Martha," the Lord answered, "you are worried and upset about many things, but few things are needed—or indeed only one. Mary has chosen what is better, and it will not be taken away from her."
Luke 10: 38-42

2. When we rely on our own soul = Eternal separation from God.

Allowing our priorities to overtake God's ultimate priorities in our lives is saying that we no longer want Jesus on the throne of our life. We are saying to Him that we think we know better how to manage our time, so we take the seat as the king in our own lives. This not only opens life up to destruction and chaos again, but eternal separation from God is imminent, since God is no longer your Lord.

3. When we rely on our own mind = ...trouble

Our minds are so inferior to the all-knowing God. God is so much more for my good than I even am and knows what is best for me, far more than I know what's best for me.

> "For my thoughts are not your thoughts, neither are your ways my ways," declares the Lord.
> "As the heavens are higher than the earth, so are my ways higher than your ways and my thoughts than your thoughts."
> Isaiah 55:8-9

By keeping the ultimate priorities first, we not only get to experience the fullness of God's goodness for ourselves, but get to carry His goodness and love to those around us, to the ends of the earth. Jesus has called every one of our names (those of us that accept Jesus as Lord), and it is up to us to respond to that call. Don't miss out on the goodness Jesus has for you by settling for the rubbish of the world. Recognize that every yes has a cost, whether that yes is to Jesus or to the ways of the world. Be conscious of what you say "yes" and "no" to, and ask God to begin to further align your decisions with His heart.

> "Commit your way to the Lord; trust in him and he will do this: He will make your righteous reward shine like the dawn, your vindication like the noonday sun."
> Psalm 37:5-6

Chapter 10 - Songs

Glorious Day, by: Passion Music, Kristian Stanfill

Same God, by: Elevation Worship, Jonsal Barrientes

Sails, by: Pat Barrett, Steffany Gretzinger, Amanda Cook

Goodness of God, by: Bethel Music, Jenn Johnson

Champion, by: Bethel Music, Dante Bowe

Chapter 11

Whole Hearted

"Is Jesus worth it all?"

Each year in January, I pray for a word or theme for the upcoming adventures that await, and I have learned that God speaks most clearly when we earnestly seek His voice and counsel with our whole heart.

> "If you look for me wholeheartedly, you will find me."
> Jeremiah 29:13 NLT

One year, the word God pressed on my heart was "all."

At first, I truly felt I had already given my all for Jesus, but boy was I wrong. Although Jesus is and always will be, on the throne of my heart and life, I will continue to have things of my flesh that strive for the throne. Being obedient to God's word for me meant rejecting the things that are not of Him and surrendering even the good things that can become idols in my life at the feet of Jesus.

"All" included my healthy hobbies, my unhealthy distraction, my money, my career, my time, my talents, my family, and my relationships. It meant all my comfort, all my independence. God was positioning my life to go from selfish independence in my own worldly comforts to complete dependence on His heavenly provision. God wanted my whole heart.

> "I will give them a heart to know that I am the Lord, and they shall be my people and I will be their God, for they shall return to me with their whole heart."
> Jeremiah 24:7 ESV

Full surrender to God means putting down our idols, truly proclaiming Jesus as Lord, and picking up the gifts He has given us to glorify His name. Surrender does not mean you are giving up all your hobbies and healthy habits. It means that they are being recognized as important, but not ultimate. That although the good things in your life have their place, they are not on the throne.

Put On the New Self

"If then you have been raised with Christ, seek

the things that are above, where Christ is, seated at the right hand of God. Set your minds on things that are above, not on things that are on earth. For you have died, and your life is hidden with Christ in God."
Colossians 3:1-3 ESV

Surrender requires looking inward for the nasty bits that have crept into your ultimate or most important priorities. So step one: Identify your idol(s). On the next page is a list of common things that can turn into idols or expose our true idols. Highlight or underline any that resonate with you and write in any I have missed in the section labeled "Other."

Self: Pride, Independence, Intellect, Health, Approval, Image, Appearance, Success, Achievement, Comparison, Fame, Identity, Status, Ego

Comfort: Safety, Security, Fear, Worry, Prosperity, Provision, Selfishness, Job, Emotions

Religion: Legalism, Rules, Arrogance, Haughtiness, Knowledge, Miracles, Signs, Wonders, gods, Rituals

Relationships: Family, Spouse, Partner, Kids, Romantic Relationship, Mentor, Influences, Celebrities, Friends, Hatred, Bitterness, Envy, People-Pleasing, Fantasy

Material Idols: Food Abuse, Substance Abuse, Money/Wealth, Entertainment (Netflix, Social Media, Video Games, etc.), Consumerism

Other: _____

Now step two: Remove and replace your idol(s). Many of the potential idols (or fruit of idols) listed above are actually good things in nature, but don't deserve the throne. Dig into what scripture says about the specific idols you highlighted or underlined. Allow Jesus and His word to speak into your idols so they can be removed and replaced by His truth. Christians seek the things of God and place their desires and affections on things outside this world, things above. Because our lives are secure in Christ, we live for Him and not for ourselves. This is not to earn salvation, but to show gratitude and love for what He has done for us. In scripture, we see that removing our idols is the only way to have Jesus front and center of our lives. Replacing our idols with Jesus and His truth is the only way we can be wholehearted in our pursuit of Jesus. This is what it looks like to put aside the world and seek God.

> "And you, my son Solomon, acknowledge the God of your father, and serve him with wholehearted devotion and with a willing mind, for the Lord searches every heart and understands every desire and every thought. If you seek him, he will be found by you; but if you forsake him, he will reject you forever."
> 1 Chronicles 28:9

While I write this portion, I am sitting in Kathmandu, Nepal about to head back to America in just a few hours. As I reflect on all that God has done with my "yes" to Him so far, and the adventures I got to take part in this particular trip as we shared the gospel here, I feel most in line with the purpose God has put on my heart:

To enjoy God's grace and extend His glory!

Nepal, which is primarily a Hindu and Buddhist country, is filled with persecution and darkness, but I got to see the light of Jesus change hearts and lives before my eyes. When we trekked to the unreached villages deep in the Himalayan mountains, we got to proclaim the good news of Jesus and give testimony to how God is moving throughout the region and world. We saw people put their faith and trust in Jesus and tangibly see the light of Jesus impact their hearts almost immediately. We also got to baptize 19 of our new brothers and sisters in Christ, worship the name of Jesus on the mountaintops, and read the bible to people who have never heard it before.
It was all so beautiful, so pure, and all so simple. We were simply obedient to the words of Jesus, and He did the rest.

"Therefore go and make disciples of all nations, baptizing them in the name of the Father and of the Son and of the Holy Spirit, and teaching them to obey everything I have commanded you. And surely I am with you always, to the very end of the age."
Matthew 28:19-20

The key that shifted my life from checking the Christian box to living a life surrendered to Jesus was my joyful worship to Him alone. When my heart of worship shifted towards Jesus, my heart broke for the things Jesus' heart broke for. As a result, the pull and power of potential idols in my life diminished and my heart grew in excitement about the things Jesus is excited about. My courage was strengthened by the words Jesus has spoken over my life. My mind was transformed by the truths of Jesus. My lens of who Jesus is became more clear and grew my faith. My grown faith led to me having the confidence to put my joyful "yes" on the table to a God that is for my good. And my yes on the table was all it took for Jesus to align my life for His purposes.

My purpose became defined by Jesus' words - to "go and make disciples of all nations." That is when the weight and urgency of this command started to really set into my heart.

"He said to them, 'Go into all the world and preach the gospel to all creation.'"
Mark 16:15

THE URGENT

[1] In 2023, it is now estimated that the world population has hit 8,000,000,000 people! That is 8 billion... with nine zeros. It is hard to grasp a number that large, especially when each individual human counted is an intricate human life, just as valuable as yours or mine. According to The Joshua Project, an organization that tracks global data, of these 8 billion people, it is estimated that 32% of the world population claims to be Christian. And of that 32%, only about 12% are estimated to be living as Christ-followers instead of box checkers (a gap that desperately needs to be filled).

The remaining 68% of people on earth, people that are not Christian, have either heard the gospel of Jesus and not responded to it (42% of the total population), or have never heard

---

1. worldometers.info

the gospel of Jesus before (26% of the total population). To put this in numbers, 2.56 billion people claim to be Christian, 3.36 billion people have heard and not responded to the gospel of Jesus, and 2.08 billion people have never even heard about Jesus before in their life.

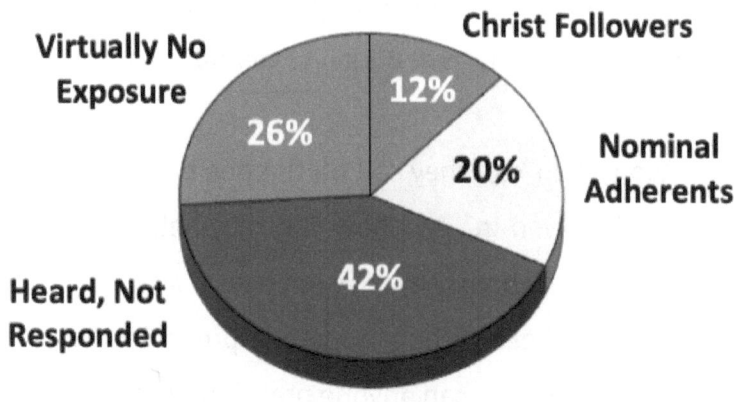

Status of World Evangelization

I understand that other religions or the rejection of God altogether are going to be choices that humans make, and my heart does break for these people. We are called to press into them and love on them as Jesus would. But the overwhelmingly heartbreaking fact is that over 2,080,000,000 people could potentially live an entire lifetime and never even hear about the good news of Jesus.[2]

---

2. joshuaproject.net

These people could live and die never having another Christian share the best news in life with them, altering their eternity. This large group is called the "unreached" because of the tragedy that it is mere logistical difficulty, political persecution, cultural barriers, or language difference that stop these people from hearing about Jesus. If they never hear about Jesus, if no one ever goes to them, they will never have the choice to call Jesus their Lord, and receive His gift of eternal life with Him.

> "How, then, can they call on the one they have not believed in? And how can they believe in the one of whom they have not heard? And how can they hear without someone preaching to them? And how can anyone preach unless they are sent?
> As it is written: "How beautiful are the feet of those who bring good news!"
> But not all the Israelites accepted the good news. For Isaiah says, "Lord, who has believed our message?"
> Consequently, faith comes from hearing the message, and the message is heard through the word about Christ."
> Romans 10:14-17

The Church is vast, strong, and resourced, but in reaching the unreached people of the planet, statistics show we are half-hearted. We allow the statistics to bounce off our rigid hearts because we are usually far enough removed from the reality of the heartbreak that people on the planet don't know they have a Savior. The Great Commission, what Matthew 28 is commonly referred to as, has hit walls of resistance, and huge chunks of the Church have settled or stopped pressing on toward the mission of making Christ known throughout all of creation.

I do not want to make light of the walls. This final portion of people that we need to get the gospel to is unreached for a reason. There are steep political barriers, logistical difficulties, language and cultural gaps, and safety or even life-threatening concerns, but we must not let the struggle of the mission allow our hearts to grow cold. We must keep praying, resourcing, teaching, and going.

I will not claim to have all the answers to completing the great commission. I do know that equipping the small number of indigenous people that already live in these hard-to-reach places is one of the most effective ways to spread the gospel in these areas, but our mission, commanded by Jesus, is an all-hands-on-deck priority. The Church is meant to pray, teach, resource, and go. As the global Church, we see a lack of prioritization for the latter two.

The Joshua Project and an organization called [3] The Traveling Team also compiled data on the finances of the global Church, and their findings are eye-opening. The estimated annual income for all Church members is around $53 trillion dollars ($53,000,000,000,000). Of that, $896 billion dollars (about 1.7%) of the Church member's annual income is given to the Church as a whole. Most of that portion (82% of the $896 billion) ends up going to the church's respective local facilities and local ministries while 12.2% goes to local evangelical ministries in Christian nations and only 5.8% goes to anything missions related, and this percentage is declining.

Of that small 5.8% (~$52 billion of $896 billion) that goes towards anything missions related, only 1.8% of this money goes toward efforts and work amongst the unreached people annually (~$9 million of $52 billion). That might sound like a lot, but for context, for every $100,000 that Christians make, only $1.70 is given to the unreached.

That is wild to me.

---

3. thetravelingteam.org/money-and-missions

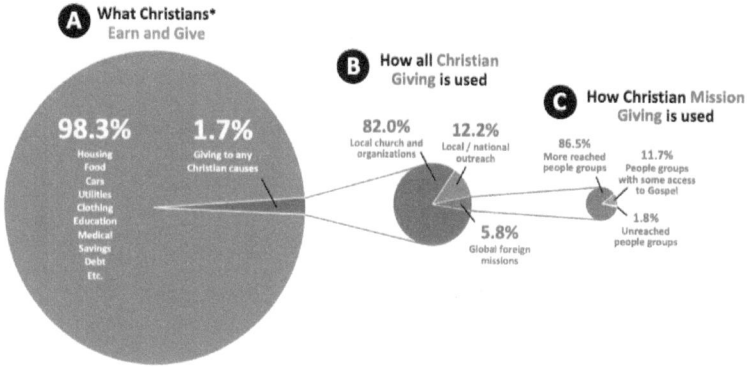

Missions & Money

Now back in Atlanta, I'm sitting here in a coffee shop writing this portion after just having spent $11 on 2 lattes for my wife and me, and am continually recognizing with conviction that my spending reflects my priorities. Our finances reflect our worship. Enjoy the blessing of a warm latte, but know that we need to activate our finances to the will of God, His people knowing Him.

Because of this, my wife and I have decided to be more diligent in how we budget, especially around how we give. We give to our local church, and it is amazing and good, but it's just a start. We continually pray for our own hearts to grow in generosity, because we want our finances to be worship to Jesus. Additionally, we have been more strategic in engaging our finances directly for the revival of unreached people groups by supporting organizations and specific missionaries that need financial help.

Our treasures in life, the things we hold close to us, need to align with our worship to Jesus by being activated towards God's work here on earth. That is how we can have eternal impact, heavenly treasures, with our temporary earthly treasure.

Treasures in Heaven

"Do not store up for yourselves treasures on earth, where moths and vermin destroy, and where thieves break in and steal. But store up for yourselves treasures in heaven, where moths and vermin do not destroy, and where thieves do not break in and steal. For where your treasure is, there your heart will be also. Matthew 6:19-21

The bottom line, we need more of our cash spent on unreached missions and less on us. Our holistic neglect of giving to our unreached brothers and sisters is one of the greatest tragedies that we as a Church should call out and repent of. But amidst this tragedy, there is opportunity like never before.

The 21st Century

We live in a generation that is unlike any other. Sure there is craziness, more distraction, and new unique hurdles, but there is also incredible innovation, opportunity, and capability that generations of the past never had. The reality of reaching every person on the planet with the gospel is more possible now than it ever has been throughout history!

When I was growing up, I never fancied history class, but every once in a while found inspiration in the people that changed the world! What I now see more clearly in innovation, technological advances, and global shifts is not the humans that lead or invented them, but God's hand.

Yes, the Wright brothers invented the airplane in 1903. What a huge innovation, but zoom out. God create Wilbur and Orville Wright! What if God's plan to give these brothers the minds to make these hunks of metal soar through the air was not for us to vacation in the Bahamas, but rather to unite the Church like never before?

Now, unlike any other time, you can get on a plane and circle the entire globe in just a couple of days. My selfishness wants to go travel and see all of creation with this ability! But what if God wants His gift of airplanes to us to be less for vacationing and more for activation of His will? Taking vacations and seeing creation isn't bad, we just need to steward our gift well. What if for every vacation I had, I went on a trip to share the gospel in the less Christian-populated areas, or used those funds to support missionaries going to places that don't know Jesus yet?

We already talked about the smartphone in chapter 1 but again, maybe the iPhone was not created by Jobs and Wozniak merely to post cat-filtered selfies of yourself on Instagram. Maybe God gave Jobs and Wozniak the minds to create such a device of connectivity and digitalization to connect people and churches beyond our borders.

See if you can see God's hand in these inventions throughout history:

The Wheel: 3500 BC
The Compass: 200 BC
Printing Press: 1440
Steam Engine: 1698
Indoor plumbing: early 1800s
Steam-Powered Train: 1804
Telephone: 1876
Electric light: 1879
Cars: 1886
Cameras: 1888
Radio: 1895

Airplanes: 1903

Television: 1926

Audiobooks: 1932

The Computer: 1939

The Internet: 1965

Cellphones: 1973

Personal computers: 1981

The World Wide Web: 1991

GPS Navigation: 1993

eReaders / eBooks: 1997

Facebook/Social Media: 2004

iPhone: 2007

Technologies are only growing more rapidly by the day and creating more opportunities than ever. What about newer innovations like the metaverse or digital decentralized currencies? What about the newer norm and ability to work fully remotely anywhere in the world? How about the plethora of data we have for literally everything in this information age? With the lens of truth, can you see God's plan for these innovations instead of just man's?

A second spectacular fact about the day and age we live in is the progress and future of bible translation. An organization called illumiNations has brought together many of the global efforts in bible translation, and due to the unity and funding of this organization, they are on track to have fully translated the bible into every single language on the planet by 2033![4] Can you believe that! Lord willing, you and I and I will be alive to see the words of Jesus available to every person on the planet in just 10 years (since writing this book in 2023)! After that, its just logistics and evangelism. All that will be required is the "yes" of Christians to go share the gospel with these people.

People that have not had the opportunity to know Jesus yet deserve to be told of their Savior. Our efforts as the global Church need to prioritize this mission and our personal lives need to be spurred to action for this mission. Jesus says that the "harvest" is plentiful, that there are ripe hearts ready to be told of the good news of Jesus. People are thirsting to know their Savior! But we have a labor shortage of Christians willing to be sent into the harvest.

The Harvest Is Plentiful, the Laborers Few

"And Jesus went throughout all the cities and villages, teaching in their synagogues and proclaiming the gospel of the kingdom and healing every disease and every affliction. When he

---

4. https://illuminations.bible/

saw the crowds, he had compassion for them, because they were harassed and helpless, like sheep without a shepherd. Then he said to his disciples, "The harvest is plentiful, but the laborers are few; therefore pray earnestly to the Lord of the harvest to send out laborers into his harvest."
Matthew 9:35-38 ESV

Today, pray for the Church to be spurred to action to send laborers into the harvest and resource initiatives already happening in unreached parts of the world. Let this mission of Jesus be prevalent in your prayer, your giving, your mindset, and in your life. Surrender any idols consuming your allegiance. Break off parts of your life that are not of God and pick up the mission Jesus has called and commanded all of us to step into. Align your whole heart with Jesus and let your heart grow in compassion for what Jesus has compassion for.

The Church is mighty, resourced, and capable. We just need better stewardship and more whole-hearted laborers.
Will you be one that says "yes Lord" and gives it all to Jesus?

"Yes, Lord, walking in the way of your laws, we wait for you; your name and renown are the desire of our hearts."
Isaiah 26:8

Chapter 11 - Songs

Whole Heart (Hold Me Now), by: Hillsong UNITED

Seated On High, by: The Belonging Co, Andrew Holt

Pursue / All I Need Is You, by: Hillsong Worship, Hillsong Young & Free

Praise Upon Praise, by: Pat Barrett

CHAPTER 12

The Challenge

"Give it all."

"For the time is coming when people will not endure sound teaching, but having itching ears they will accumulate for themselves teachers to suit their own passions, and will turn away from listening to the truth and wander off into myths."
2 Timothy 4:3-4 ESV

To follow Jesus, say yes to Him and His word in its entirety. To only submit to some of the Word of God and pretend certain books or verses in the Bible don't exist, or to reject certain pieces of scripture, is to reject God's Word and Jesus entirely. You can easily find a pastor or speaker to suit your personal "Jesus" and teach you only the things you want to hear, but this is a belligerent way to approach the throne of God and His Word. I guarantee you can find a version of the gospel to fit your wants and needs by twisting or avoiding certain scripture, but this is one of the most destructive things you can do to yourself. Because there is only one Jesus who sits on the throne, who has already spoken, whose words are alive and active, and who is worthy of your heart of worship.

Our only 2 options then are to accept Jesus for who He says He is, not who we want Him to be, or reject Him. This is not a decision that is confirmed only by our words, but by our hearts, by our actions.

> **"As water reflects the face, so one's life reflects the heart."**
> **Proverbs 27:19**

Be aware that the Word of God and a relationship with Jesus will change your life and your heart. It will change who you are as a person. It will change your decisions, your outlooks, and your perspectives.

Having the words of the Creator of the universe realign your life with its original design is the whole point of following Jesus. If you are resisting the prompts that God puts on your heart through His Word, then you are resisting Jesus. I do not always get this right myself, but when I see resistance in my life to bend to the will of the Lord, I start with prayer for my heart to soften. I ask God to widen my perspective, to remind me of my purpose, and I take my eyes off of myself and put them back on Jesus. Because it is likely that my resistance is really underlying pride and selfishness trying to take back the throne of my heart, or that I am clinging onto something of this world too tightly.

The only other alternative to continue to believe that the Word of God is true while allowing your life to continue in darkness and resist the transformation God is trying to conduct in your life is to twist scripture. Please do not do this, I beg you. Allow your life to be transformed by scripture, not the other way around. God is in the business of changing lives for your good and His glory, if you let Him.

> "And we know that for those who love God all things work together for good, for those who are called according to his purpose."
> Romans 8:28 ESV

I know that no human alive today will get God's word 100% correct. To say that we have no faults in our theology would be ignorant. But the point is to not make Christianity a thing that comfortably fits your life and agenda as opposed to allowing it to be a catalyst for change in your life.

Walking with Jesus is often uncomfortable and will stretch and test you. Sit under biblical leadership that challenges you and isn't afraid of delving into the tough questions and parts of the Bible. Find a community that truly wants to grow in loving righteousness and will not settle for lukewarm faith. Take time to process the word of God, and along with its beauty and easy truths, allow its difficult truths to sink deep into your heart. Following Jesus is the hardest and most life-changing thing that will happen to you during your short time here on earth, so if "your Jesus" perfectly fits into a comfortable mold created by worldly truths, then you are following a myth, not Jesus.

I say all of this out of love and want to reiterate, the only way to live a life with Jesus is to allow your heart to be changed and captured by God's Word so He may activate you to help bring the kingdom of heaven to earth. For that to happen, you need Jesus fervently and sincerely on the throne of your heart of worship. Jesus has all the authority in heaven and on earth and through His teaching, we see His heart for our lives. He calls us to know and reflect Him, to do the will of His Father (also our Father) in heaven.

²¹ "Not everyone who says to me, 'Lord, Lord,' will enter the kingdom of heaven, but only the one who does the will of my Father who is in heaven. ²² Many will say to me on that day, 'Lord, Lord, did we not prophesy in your name and in your name drive out demons and in your name perform many miracles?' ²³ Then I will tell them plainly, 'I never knew you. Away from me, you evildoers!'

²⁴ "Therefore everyone who hears these words of mine and puts them into practice is like a wise man who built his house on the rock. ²⁵ The rain came down, the streams rose, and the winds blew and beat against that house; yet it did not fall, because it had its foundation on the rock. ²⁶ But everyone who hears these words of mine and does not put them into practice is like a foolish man who built his house on sand. ²⁷ The rain came down, the streams rose, and the winds blew and beat against that house, and it fell with a great crash."

²⁸ When Jesus had finished saying these things,

the crowds were amazed at his teaching, [29] because he taught as one who had authority, and not as their teachers of the law.
Matthew 7:21-29

When I was 24 years old, I read the book [1] *Radical* by David Platt. It is a book that challenged me to grow in my walk with Jesus and to wrestle with tough scripture. It didn't shy away from the difficult words of Jesus that we are called to say "yes" to as believers, and it inspired me to put my faith into action.

It helped activate some of the atrophied muscles I was not utilizing in my daily walk with Jesus and inspired me to take God's word seriously and make some big life changes because of it. I highly recommend giving Radical a read if you would like to dig even deeper into your relationship with Jesus. At the end of the book, David poses some challenges after spending so much time delving into scriptural truths. I would like to do the same. Now that we have unpacked some central points of scripture, how will the Word of God change our lives? How will God change your life?

I have included a contract that has some prayer points and commitments if you are serious about giving the reins of your

---

1. Radical, David Platt

heart to Jesus. Pray through each item, and when you are ready, write down a commitment (or use the one included) that you would like to make to grow closer to Jesus. I promise you will not regret giving Jesus more of your heart.

The aim of my life is, and I encourage the aim of yours to be, the desire to joyfully serve the Lord with my whole heart. To live a worshipful life so that at the end of my days, Jesus will say these words found in Matthew 25 to me with a full embrace. **"Well done, good and faithful servant."**

> "His master replied, 'Well done, good and faithful servant! You have been faithful with a few things; I will put you in charge of many things. Come and share your master's happiness!'"
> Matthew 25:21

As the Creator who made you, God perfectly knows your purpose. He holds your identity.

As Father, He is ready and eager to train you and walk with you. He has compassion and grace in your weakness and champions your strengths as you grow. As Shepherd, He has His hand on your life. He pursues you with zeal, guides you in murky terrain, and is always available as the wonderful counselor to you. As King Jesus, your life has been commanded to be on mission, a mission that is full of joy and trial. God is for your good and with you always. He has a plan for you and this King is at the door of your life knocking. Jesus wants to do life with you!

What will your response be to the voice of the King of kings?

> "Here I am! I stand at the door and knock. If anyone hears my voice and opens the door, I will come in and eat with that person, and they with me."
> Revelations 3:20

The Challenge

I went too many years before I took action on the things the Bible advises and commands us as followers of Jesus to take seriously. I urge you to make a commitment to allow Jesus onto the throne of your life and step into action. These are not all actions that are one and done, but I challenge you to look at each of these challenges and commit to integrating them into your life priorities.

If you go to my Linktree (https://linktr.ee/bryankeller) or scan the QR code you can print out this challenge and commitment document and put it somewhere you will see it frequently. Choose one challenge every week to emphasize and as God molds your heart to look like His, you will transform to look more like Jesus.

SCAN LINKTREE QR CODE HERE:

1. Fill your life with truth

- Read the entire bible and fall in love with God (I recommend chronological order).

- Find a spiritual mentor that can pour wisdom into you.

2. Share that truth with others

- Find a person you can disciple in their walk with Jesus and pour into them.

- Share the good news of Jesus with someone that does not yet call Jesus Lord.

- Press into a community that follows Jesus and do life with them.

3. Give God the glory

- Identify and hone your God-given gifts.

- Use your gifts to glorify God.

4. Soften your heart

- Identify the brokenness in humanity that God has burdened your heart with.

- Proclaim that God is good and wants to use your life to help bring the kingdom of heaven to earth in that area of brokenness.

5. Surrender idols

- Write out your ultimate priorities, important priorities, and unimportant time suckers then set boundaries on time suckers.

- Surrender the idol currently occupying or most frequently grasping for the throne of your heart.

6. Burst your bubble

- Place yourself in an unfamiliar context where you can be a light to people that do not know who Jesus is.

- Pray for the Church to be spurred to action amidst a ripe harvest, with a willing heart to be the answer to that prayer.

- Identify what truths in scripture make you uncomfortable and learn more about them.

7. Conquer fear

- Identify a fear that the enemy has used to hold you back and go to God's Word for courage and truth to overcome it.

- Break off the weight of any sin that you have been carrying far too long by confessing it to God and to a person you trust.

- Walk in courage knowing your identity in Christ, filled with the Holy Spirit.

8. Rest in Jesus

- Dwell in the presence of God and listen to His voice.

- Spend time in the quiet place of prayer with Jesus and pour out your heart to Him.

- Allow Jesus to fill your desires with what God desires.

9. Activate your love

- Live in pursuit of Jesus and His will.

- Love people well. (Read Romans 12)

"Love must be sincere. Hate what is evil; cling to what is good. Be devoted to one another in love. Honor one another above yourselves."
Romans 12:9-10

10. Exalt the King of kings with your life through a Heart of Worship!

Drive a stake in the ground! Fill in and read out loud the following prayer and surrender the throne of your heart to Jesus if you haven't done so already. Put this day on your calendar as a day of celebration that you can look back on each year to come.

The Commitment

"Jesus, you are worthy of it all. You are the only one that deserves my heart of worship. You are the only one that deserves the throne of my heart.

On _____ (date), I _____ (name) give the throne of my heart to you, Jesus. I commit to walking in the ways you have commanded and I surrender my life to bring glory to your name. Jesus, mold my life to reflect my allegiance to you in all that I do, that I may go and make disciples amongst people that do not yet know you. I love you with all my heart, mind, and soul, and I pray that you use my 'yes' to help fulfill your purposes in heaven and on earth.

Let it be so."

"Oh come, let us sing to the Lord; let us make a joyful noise to the rock of our salvation!
Let us come into his presence with thanksgiving; let us make a joyful noise to him with songs of praise!
For the Lord is a great God, and a great King above all gods.
In his hand are the depths of the earth; the heights of the mountains are his also.
The sea is his, for he made it, and his hands formed the dry land.
Oh come, let us worship and bow down; let us kneel before the Lord, our Maker!
For he is our God, and we are the people of his pasture, and the sheep of his hand."
Psalm 95:1-7 ESV

Chapter 12 - Songs

Worthy of It All, by: Lindy Cofer, Circuit Rider Music

Gratitude, by: Brandon Lake

Always Good, by: Bethel Music, Hannah McClure

Missionary Anthem, by: YWAM Kona Music, Seth Yates

The Heart Of Worship, by: Passion, Matt Redman

Conclusion
Worship / Proskuneo / Προσκυνεὼ

As discussed, worship is so much more than singing songs. Worship is everything you do in life, and living with a heart of worship aligned with Jesus is the greatest joy of our days on this planet. Thank you for taking the time to read Heart of Worship. My hope is that the content discussed in this book spurs you to action as a follower of Jesus today, and for the rest of your life. One last resource to leave you with is a message by [1] Francis Chan called the "Rope Illustration." Give it a google and watch the 4ish minute Youtube video of a section of Francis Chan's message.

The video drives home the point better than words can, but the gist is that life is short and eternity is long, so lets use our limited time here on earth in a way that glorifies God through a life of surrender to Him. God used to dwell in Jewish temples

---

1. Rope Illustration, Francis Chan

made by man, but now God lives inside of you and I, His people, His church. We no longer have to go somewhere to worship, our lives are worship to Jesus.

In Hebrews 11, we see a long list of devout men and women of faith including Abraham, Issac, Jacob, Moses, Rahab, David, and many others that lived a life of faith, aligned and surrendered to the Lord. A life with a heart of worship. In the next chapter, Hebrews 12, we then get to see that these same men and women of the past are cheering us on in heaven to our finish line.

> "Therefore, since we are surrounded by such a great cloud of witnesses, let us throw off everything that hinders and the sin that so easily entangles. And let us run with perseverance the race marked out for us, fixing our eyes on Jesus, the pioneer and perfecter of faith. For the joy set before him he endured the cross, scorning its shame, and sat down at the right hand of the throne of God. Consider him who endured such opposition from sinners, so that you will not grow weary and lose heart."
> Hebrews 12:1-3

These witnesses know the earthly struggle, but prevailed. They know the trial of the enemy, but remained faithful. They know the distraction of idols, but decided to worship Jesus with their life. With eyes fixed on Jesus, know that Jesus Himself has been in your shoes of trial too. He knows the ups and downs of life on earth. Let the example of Jesus spur on your faith continually as you walk this life. Do not grow weary and lose heart. Reflect Jesus to the world around you with joy, through a heart of worship.

> "Therefore, since we are receiving a kingdom that cannot be shaken, let us be thankful, and so worship God acceptably with reverence and awe, for our 'God is a consuming fire.'"
> Hebrews 12:28-29

SHARE THE LOVE

"A REVIEW IS WORTH 1000 THANK YOUS"

If you enjoyed the book, it would mean the world to me if you shared it with someone you think would enjoy reading it and if you left a 5-star review on Amazon. I have not published much yet, but I know positive reviews help the algorithm boost your book so it can impact more readers. By leaving your review, you would help me tremendously on that mission! Lastly, here is my Linktree again which I will continue to update with any future resources and where you can stay connected with me via email or text.

Thank you for reading & for all of your support,

Bryan Keller

HEART OF WORSHIP RESOURCES:

https://linktr.ee/bryankeller

Includes:

- "Heart of Worship" Book - Share & Review Link
- "Heart of Worship" Playlists
- "Heart of Worship – Instrumental" Playlists
- "Challenge / Commitment" PDF Print Out
- "Chronological Bible Reading Plan" PDF Print Out
- "Heart of Worship" Audiobook Link

+ more to come!

Acknowledgments

Thank you to all my friends and family that helped make this book a reality!

To my Bible study guys throughout the years, it has been an honor to run the race of life and grow in the ways of Jesus alongside you all. Thank you to my mentors and leaders for teaching and guiding me. Your ear and wisdom means more to mean than you know. Thank you mom and dad for being such great examples of how to live lives submitted to Jesus. I am the man I am today because of your love and support.

Thank you, Sydney, for being the most amazing wife, partner, and friend. Doing life with you is such a joy and adventure! Thank you to everyone that supported me in prayer and finances during my time with YWAM in Nepal. That trip shifted something in my heart and had such tangible fruit in Nepal and in my life. Your generosity and fragrant prayer had (and still have) amazing impact!

Thank you all for reflecting the character of Jesus in various ways to me. I have learned more about the heart of God because you all are in my life.

And last but not least, thank YOU for picking up a copy of Heart Of Worship and reading it. I hope you found value in it and share that value with those God has placed around you.

Thank you so much,

About the Author

Bryan Keller lives in Atlanta, GA with his wife Sydney where they attend and serve at The Square Church. Recognizing the heart of God for their city and the entire world, Bryan and Sydney have a heart to share the gospel through love in Atlanta and in the areas on earth that have not yet been reached with the good news of Jesus (The 10/40 window). With a bachelor's degree and passion for business, Bryan also started Keller Guitars, which helps support his family and other missionaries reach the unreached with the gospel of Jesus.

Other Notes

All Icons made free by various creators from flaticon.com:

    Cover & Ch2 Icon made by alkhalifi design

    Preface, Intro, Share The Love, & Chapters 3, 8, 9, 10, 12 Icons made by Freepik

    Ch1 Icon made by Prosymbols Premium

    Ch4 Icon made by surang

    Ch5 Icon made by iconixar

    Ch6 Icon made by msidiqf

    Ch7 Icon made by Pixel perfect

    Ch11 Icon made by Royyan Wijaya

    Conclusion Icon made by IconBaandar

Images:

    Jordan River image (Ch5), www.un.org/geospatial/content/israel-1

    Animals To Climb Tree image (Ch7), created by Hans Traxler 1976

    Be Not Afraid - Tiger painting (Ch9), created by Scott Erickson

    Status of World Evangelization image (ch11), The Joshua Project

    Missions & Money image (ch11), The Joshua Project

    worship definition image, Google (the Oxford Languages)

Dictionary

Definitions from Oxford Languages · Learn more

 wor·ship

noun

noun: **worship**

- the feeling or expression of reverence and adoration for a deity.
  "the worship of God"

  Similar: reverence | revering | worshipping | veneration | venerating

- the acts or rites that make up a formal expression of reverence for a deity; a religious ceremony or ceremonies.
  "the church was opened for public worship"

  Similar: service | church service | religious rite | religious act | prayer

- adoration or devotion comparable to religious homage, shown toward a person or principle.
  "our society's worship of teenagers"

  Similar: admiration | adulation | idolization | deification | lionization

- **ARCHAIC**
  honor given to someone in recognition of their merit.

- **BRITISH**
  used in addressing or referring to an important or high-ranking person, especially a magistrate or mayor.
  noun: **His Worship**; noun: **Your Worship**; plural noun: **Worships**
  "we were soon joined by His Worship the Mayor"

verb

verb: **worship**; 3rd person present: **worships**; past tense: **worshipped**; past participle: **worshipped**; gerund or present participle: **worshipping**; past tense: **worshiped**; past participle: **worshiped**; gerund or present participle: **worshiping**

- show reverence and adoration for (a deity); honor with religious rites.
  "the Maya built jungle pyramids to worship their gods"

  Similar: revere | reverence | venerate | pay homage to | honor | adore

- take part in a religious ceremony.
  "he went to the cathedral because he chose to worship in a spiritually inspiring building"

- treat (someone or something) with the reverence and adoration appropriate to a deity.
  "she adores her sons and they worship her"

Origin

OLD ENGLISH
weorthscipe

ENGLISH — worship
worth
-ship

Old English *weorthscipe* 'worthiness, acknowledgment of worth' (see worth, -ship).

Use over time for: worship

www.ingramcontent.com/pod-product-compliance
Lightning Source LLC
Chambersburg PA
CBHW020655060526
44119CB00068B/8